Austin's Gift

Austin's Gift

The Life of a Grateful Organ Recipient

When you are healthy, you wish for a thousand things.
When you are sick, you only wish for one thing.

by Lauren Ann Aggen

Hilton Publishing Company - Munster, Indiana

Hilton Publishing Company
1630 45th Street, Suite 103
Munster, IN 46321
219-922-4868
www.hiltonpub.com

Notice: The information in this book is a remembrance of life experiences and is true and complete to the best of the authors' and publisher's knowledge. This book should not replace, countermand, or conflict with the advice given to readers by their physicians. The authors and publisher disclaim all liability in connection with the specific personal use of any and all information provided in this book.

Grant E. Mabie, *Managing Editor*
Tammy Weaver-Stoike and Lynn Bell, *Editorial Assistance*
David E. Haan, *Layout and Design*

Publisher's Cataloging-in-Publication
(Provided by Quality Books, Inc.)

Aggen, Lauren.
    Austin's gift: the life of a grateful organ recipient/Lauren Aggen.
        p. cm.
    ISBN 978-0-9841447-6-1 (pbk.)
        1. Aggen, Lauren--Health. 2.
    Heart--Transplantation--Patients--Illinois--Biography. I. Title.
    RD598.35.T7A34 2011
    617.4'120592--dc22
                2011006952

Printed and bound in the United States of America
11 12 13 14 15 6 5 4 3 2 1

Dedication

To transplant families,
Donor families,
And for those who are waiting.
And to those who made my life a fairy tale,
Even in the worst times.

Table of Contents

Acknowledgments

Some names of people in my story have been changed
for personal reasons or to protect their privacy.

(People who made my life a fairytale even in the worst times)

Creator of Us All	God (I love you!)
Magical Storyteller	Grandpa Sumner (I miss you!)
Mysterious Gypsy	Donna (Thanks for filling my life with happiness and fun surprises.)
Queen of Hearts/King	Dr. Brown/Dr. Kauffman (Thank you for taking care of me.)
Nutcracker Godfather	Uncle George (I admire your generosity in life, and I love my Precious Moments dolls.)
Fairy Godmother	Beautiful Betty (You have the most generous heart.)
Sunflower Fairy	Mom (Thank you for being the best mom in the whole world.)
Father of the Bride	Dad (Thank you for being the best dad in the whole world.)
Superman	Dave (Thanks for being the best role model I know of.)
Peter Pan	Mark (Thanks for showing me Neverland is in my life.)
~~Evil~~ Saintly Step-Sisters	Kelsi and Kimina (What would I do without you!)
Chip and Cruella de Vil	Mr. and Mrs. Trayser (Two words….. CREAM PUFFS!!)
Belle	Winnie Rogers (Thank you for being my favorite teacher. I have learned so much from you.)

Angels of Friendship	The Teacups, Freriches, Novaks, Bondys, Subergs, Kulacks, Westerbecks, Schumakers, Paldaufs, Acevedos, Roods, and Sue Vetter (Thank you for your loving support and friendship.)
Villains	My broken valve, viruses, or any type of sickness I can catch.
The Incredibles	Chris (Thank you for saving me by sharing your blood! Thanks to all the people who came and were tested at the lab!)
And last, but not least…	
Prince Charming	My donor!

Thanks to the medical specialists who don't give up and have kept me healthy to enjoy life! A special debt of gratitude to Pediatric Associates of Barrington, who have provided excellent care and guidance for 21 years!

Thanks to my Church Family and friends for coming through in my times of need. You are awesome!

Thanks to Dr. Stacy and Rick Loukas for sharing their expertise. Thanks to all my teachers and professors. Your guidance helped prepare me for this project.

SPECIAL thanks to the Make-a Wish-Foundation, my Dream Team (Tom McClaughly, Alison Womac, and Amy Ceciliano), and Grant from Hilton Publishing Company for helping this book to be born!

Note to Readers

I am the recipient of the greatest gift ever. I received an organ from a three-month-old baby boy, whom I will call "Austin," when I was eight days old. I hope that this story will express my deepest gratitude to those families who have allowed their children to be organ donors. I feel it is important to reinforce that their gift made someone else's life possible and better. I hope that, over time, they have found some comfort knowing their child made an important difference in the lives of others.

In addition, I wanted to write this book to tell parents of children who may need a transplant that, although life may be challenging, it will still be happy! When I was born, there were no babies older than four months in Chicago who had undergone heart transplantation. At the time, my family wished they had a reference, some insight as to what they might expect, because there was so little history. Every story is different, but my story may give a little insight into the life of a child who has lived through this life-and-near-death situation.

I also wrote this book for people who don't know about transplants. I like to read stories that have medical plots, and I believe there are others who might like to get an idea of what it's like to be a child with a transplant. Ever since I was 13, I have wanted to make a difference. I hope that, by writing this book, someone's life may be saved because a hero was willing to discuss being an organ donor with his or her family, or register with their state to donate their organs to help others who need them. In gratitude to my parents, I will be a reference they were looking for when I was born, and hopefully I will be a reference for others too! For the people who are waiting for an organ, I hope you get your special gift from someone like "Austin," or from some other very special person soon.

Aggen

Each chapter in this book begins with a reference to a song I selected. Today, despite my profound hearing loss, I am obsessed with music and believe it will help you understand more about my recollections. Music reflects mood and imagination, but it also has inspired me to think positively and write these stories in this book, because often songs are associated with my memories. I hope you'll listen to the music on your digital audio players or look up the lyrics online as you read the chapters.

In addition, thanks to the foundation that makes children's dreams come true, and the people who work so hard to help others realize their wishes in spite of adversity. To the *Make a Wish Foundation* and my Dream Team, your efforts encouraged me at one of my bleakest points. Focusing on this publication helped me overcome and continue. To all of my Dream Team, my deepest thanks!

Preface

Have you ever wondered how it would feel to have someone else's heart beating in your chest? Did you just try to think about how your own heart "feels"? I can answer that, with a stethoscope, most of the time I hear the same lub-dub you would hear if you listened to your own through the tool. But I can't compare because I don't know what it would be like having my own heart! When I was born, my heart wasn't performing efficiently enough to keep me alive. If I had had to depend on my own heart, I wouldn't have seen the year 1990. People have asked me questions when they learn I have had a heart transplant. Actually, there are two responses that are the most popular. One is, "Oh yeah, my uncle had that." It usually means they know someone who had heart surgery. The other common reaction is that the person pauses; they can't think of what to say. They need time to process the idea. One time, I was with my grandmother, and one of her friends stopped to ask, "Do you really have a little boy's heart beating in you?" When I affirmed this extraordinary fact, she shook her head and said, "It's hard for me to understand, but it is a miracle." I think that is a very honest response.

"Can it fall out?" This is a common question from adults and children. One misconnection people have is that you got a new heart and that's that. The truth is, I traded certain death for a life-long medical condition. "Do you have to take medicine?" Yes, I do. Forever. "Is there anything you can't do?" I can't scuba dive, and I haven't inquired about bungee jumping. Pretty much, I can do whatever I want, and that is spectacular. Something I'd like you to remember, however: *nothing* would have been possible without my donor.

I didn't have the opportunity to live a regular life, and then receive a transplant. I sometimes wonder how different my life would have been if I hadn't *begun* with a transplant. But then I realize, I wouldn't be here if it wasn't for the extraordinary exchange of my own heart for a new-to-me one! Is it harder for someone to begin with a transplant, or would it be more difficult to grow up as a normal kid, and then, in the teen or adult years, need a transplant?

My donor didn't have the opportunity to lead a normal life either. I can't imagine what it's like to lose a loved one, especially your child. I have met donor families through my experience of volunteering for Donate Life. I haven't met anyone yet who has lost their child due to SIDS, but I'm sure I will get the goose bumps if I do.

Something that is really neat for me is that my donor's birthstone is my *favorite* gem. Could it be that the fact that I like that color has anything to do with my donor's preferences? A sapphire stone will always mean something more to me, because it reminds me of my donor. Could it be that I like it because of him? I want to make the best use of his gift and live life to the fullest. I have always been a fan of Princess Diana for her altruistic efforts. I hope to make contributions in my own small way.

1

The Chicken Pox Shot

"Not Ready To Make Nice" by Dixie Chicks

I remember, I was sitting in my second-grade class, and the nurse, Mrs. Skipper, came running through my classroom door. "Ms. Rogers, I need Lauren Aggen, right away!" Ms. Rogers cooperated in her usual perky manner. However, then I saw my mom's face behind the nurses, and she seemed very stressed. My mother said, "Lauren, bring your stuff with you." I knew that meant I wouldn't be returning to school that day.

I was standing in the hallway, when the nurse told me, once again, the dreaded reason, the same thing she had told me less than a month before. "Someone in your class went home with *chicken pox* today." I knew exactly what that meant for me. I walked to Mom's car with my head down, dreading what was now ahead of me.

I was sitting on that long, thin, cold examining table in the doctor's office. My back was touching the cold white wall, which I used to lean on. The nurse hadn't even come in, and my eyes were already filling with water. My mother stayed strong for me, watching her only daughter sob, knowing there was no way to avoid the tremendous pain that I would soon experience. I knew the process. *It was necessary to have shots to save me from the effects of chicken pox, which, while trivial for others, were life-threatening for me.* The shot had to be injected into my thigh muscle with a thick, blunt needle. The liquid that could save my life cost $1,000 per shot, and, in spite of that fact, at times the gamma globulin was in short supply. The older I got, the more medication I needed for this purpose. Also, there was a limit on how much could be injected at one site. There were times I had to get three shots in the thigh right in a row. It was extremely painful, and I could barely move my legs to walk after the injections. At the time, there was no vaccine available for chicken pox. Even now that there is, I still can't have it, because it is a live virus, and I might get sick from the vaccine because I am immunosuppressed (but more about that later).

Unbelievably, I never had an active case of chicken pox. If I had, I likely could have died. You see, when I was eight days old I received a heart transplant. My new heart is great. But transplant patients' immune systems are not very active, and any sliver, bite, infection, or virus could trick our bodies into rejecting our new hearts. Tragically, after several children with heart transplants died of complications following infection, the doctors recognized the immune response to chicken pox could lead to organ rejection. Children with heart transplants who developed chicken pox were hospitalized immediately and given intravenous gamma globulin specific for chicken pox to try to limit the effects of the virus. If I got chicken pox, my body might not be strong enough to fight it. I would be very sick . . . or dead. You can see how my view of normal everyday events changed relative to other kids. If I even saw chicken pox I knew the consequences: a painful shot and more time away from home in Chicago.

Out of the corner of my eye, I saw Diane and Sheri approaching. Diane and Sheri have been my nurses since I was a baby. Even though I thought they were the nicest people ever, my pale face began to turn red as the water ran down my cheeks, and I had a hard time breathing. "NOOOOOOOOOOOOOOOOO!" I screamed. I felt my body tense up, like my body was a rubber band and someone was pulling downward forcefully on my feet. In Diane and Sheri's hands was the object of my fear . . . the dreaded *chicken pox shot*, as I called it. The needle was too long, too thick—too painful to jab into a little girl like me.

Two other nurses came in after Diane, and I knew exactly what they were going to do. Jean and Jillian were very encouraging, but they had to hold my arms and legs down so I wouldn't move while Diane and Sheri inserted the thick needles into the muscles of my thighs.

Even though I was only so young, I remember the fear I felt when I saw that needle. Diane, Sheri, Jean, and Jillian were all very empathetic and spoke encouragingly to me. On other visits, their cheerful scrub outfits would have distracted me. Colorful frogs, fairies, princesses, Sponge Bob, or Power Rangers on smocks with bright matching pants surprised the small patients at each visit. There were stickers when you left, and sometimes temporary tattoos. They knew I loved princesses, and they would have a Snow White sticker for me when I left, to cheer me up.

Eventually, I would relax because I would get tired of making a fuss.

And that's when my left leg felt a sharp sting, like one thousand bees stinging a single spot on my leg. Then my right leg felt the same. Eventually, both thighs starting burning, as if I was in hell. The lumps were gigantic. By the next day, I would have huge bruises. In time, though, I learned that this pain would only be temporary, and that I would be stronger when I was faced with life's other challenges.

When it was all done, I had to put my pants on, which covered up my bandaging. There was no outward evidence of the traumatic shot I had received. I would always go back to our car in a wheelchair. In retrospect, this I felt was a major perk. I enjoyed being chauffeured to the car after the needle brought on those feelings of fear. Afterward, my legs felt so bruised that it was difficult to walk. It felt like a truck had dumped chunks of cement over my legs. Whenever I saw a kid with chicken pox I thought of that shot, that moment of fear. But, with time, I would learn to overcome that fear.

The older I got, the more shots I had to get at once. *I didn't want to grow up, NEVER GROW UP; I was feeling just like one of the Lost Boys in the movie "Peter Pan." Stay young forever, I thought. While I still like this idea, I am glad that I've gotten to grow up a little, and all because someone was willing to donate their loved one's organs. I wouldn't be here were it not for Austin's gift, and I want to write about my experiences as a transplant recipient so that everyone can understand the effect of his gift. Although he is gone, a part of him, literally, lives on in me.*

• • • •

Special Note

One constant battle for those who have transplants is suppressing the immune system enough so that it doesn't attack the new organ, but not too much to fight off other diseases, including cancer and bacterial or viral infections. Viruses, colds, and infections are more easily caught, and they last longer than they do in people who are not taking anti-rejection medication. Gamma globulin, if used within 24 hours of exposure, could lessen the severity of the chicken pox experience in children who need anti-rejection medications. This chapter refers to these therapeutic shots, not the vaccination now available to develop antibodies. At the time when exposure was most prevalent in kindergarten and first grade, the vaccinations were new and many fellow students had not had them. As time passed, there were less exposures and less need for the nasty gamma globulin shots, in part because so many families co-operated with varicella immunizations.

2
Giving and Receiving
"Superman" by Five for Fighting

Contrasts to my own story were revealed during a volunteer-training group meeting for organ donor awareness with other transplant recipients and donor families. I didn't know anyone in my group. People were sharing their stories of how they received a transplant, or the story of their family member becoming a donor. The transplant recipient who cried telling his story for the first time, relating his gratitude to a group that included a mother whose five-year-old son was a donor, moved me. A Hispanic man tearfully told his story of receiving an organ. It was so touching when he talked about the fact that, if it weren't for his donor, he would have never met his newborn daughter. He said he is reminded every day when he sees his daughter's face to be thankful for organ donation. I'm not much of a crier at emotional stuff like this, but my eyes were a little watery.

Next, another mother began to tell her experience. She was young and pretty, but she looked very tired. Her eyes had a sad look. She cried and wanted to say something, but she couldn't. "I appreciate everyone sharing stories, but . . ." She couldn't continue; the pain was too new. She cried softly.

Her husband was in the other group, with my mom and Uncle Dan. This gentle, soft-spoken man was able to tell the story of his son, who was a donor. My mom told me about it later; she knew that the man in her group was married to the lady who was constantly trying to fight back her tears in my group, because my mom chatted with her later. "It happened less than a year ago," he said, "when my wife was driving her car, with our five-year old son in the backseat. Suddenly another car hit theirs head on. When my wife got out of the car, she tried to get our boy out of the backseat, but he was limp and not responsive." He expressed how the mother felt responsible for her son's death just because she was driving the car, even though she was not at fault. The man continued, "We were very happy to hear that one of our son's organs went to a man who lived his life helping children. It seems like a complete circle, and we feel it is very special that our son could return the favor by sharing his organs to help this man who had dedicated himself to helping children. It was amazing to hear the number of people he saved or helped. It helped us feel our son had a purpose."

On the car ride home from the training, I once again thought about the lady whose son died, and wondered if my donor's mom was like her. Would my donor's family feel comfort from my story? How do they imagine their son: as a baby, or the man they dreamed he'd become? Then my brain flashed back to my memory of the loving family I imagined was the source of my marvelous gift. I realize my reason for this scenario is that it gives me a comfortable feeling to believe that Austin was part of a loving family. I know the story will sound a little typecast. The nationality, race, and sex of my donor are not important. It doesn't matter which holidays my donor family do or don't celebrate. They gave me a chance of life, and that is the most generous thing anyone can do.

What situation allows another's heart to sustain my life? It can't be a crushing blow to the chest, as a car accident with chest injury. It *could* be an accident as a result of a gunshot, or impact to the brain. It wouldn't be from a disease, but it could be a birth defect such an anecephalic baby (one born without a brain.). What could cause a baby's death that wouldn't affect his heart but would allow his heart to work in my body? In the case of my donor, it was Sudden Infant Death Syndrome.

3
Temporary Home
"Silent Night" by Libera

This is my rendition of a tragic Christmas for one family in Austin, Texas: Austin's family. I have no way of knowing, but this is how I think it might have been:

Date: December 29, 1989

Her wavy brunette locks bounced against the soft maroon robe that the children gave their Mom for Christmas. Tiptoeing as gracefully as an angel to the bedroom next door, her beautiful smile shone once her entrance into the peaceful sky-blue room was completed. Her heart pounded more once she saw the mobile dangling above her newborn, sleeping peacefully. The western stars mobile was playing a delightful lullaby. She adored looking at her child. He didn't have to do anything; he was *loved*. She was totally captivated by his precious innocence. She gently laid her hand against his chest, to savor the heartbeat of the tiny, sleeping three-month-old. So peaceful. So quiet. So still! Too still. . . .

• • • •

Four days earlier: December 25, 1989

A cry is heard, coming from down the hall. The mother of three moves gracefully, as she puts on her ragged robe torn by the dog, and walks toward the nursery. Her new son has his mother's smile, which has nothing to do with her adoration of him. He gives her a sweet grin when she looks at him, for he knows she brings comfort. She picks him up, and is making silly faces for him to contemplate. He is just three months old, the age when many babies develop a sense of recognition and are a little curious about the five senses—especially touch. He has dark hair like his mother, and has been blessed with his grandfather's magnificent blue eyes.

His mother takes him to her room, where everything is crazy, almost out of control, but festive, happy, and alive. The twins beg for permission to begin opening presents. They are so excited to have a new brother to celebrate with this Christmas. The tall, dark, and handsome father scoops one kid in each arm and takes them on a "superman" ride down the stairs as the twins manage to put their arms straight out in front of their faces. The mother, carrying her newborn in her arms, has been anticipating the excitement as she planned for this Christmas morning of opening presents with her three children.

"This one is for *Austin*!!" the girl says. "It's from *me*!" She gently hands the baby a box that is bigger than the baby himself. Inside the box is a large piece of paper with a kiddy drawing on it—a drawing of the family.

"That's very sweet of you, Morgan," compliments her mother.

After kissing their brother on the forehead, the twins are ready to open their presents.

"It's a *Caterpillar bulldozer*! Yes, just what I wanted!" says Tommy.

"Tommy!" Morgan exclaims. "Look what I got! An *Easy Bake oven*!" She shows it off to her unimpressed brother, who rolls his eyes in anxious impatience to get back to his own treasures. "I can make brownies for you, or chocolate chip cookies!" With that, Tommy is more accepting of his sister's joy.

The husband surprises his wife with a necklace, which he pulls out of his pocket and slips around her neck. She recognizes exactly what this necklace represents. Three birthstones stacked like a snowman, except the stones are all the same size. The top two stones are both brilliant round diamonds to represent the twins' April birthday. On the bottom of the two upper round diamonds was a single sapphire, representing Austin's birth in September of this year.

• • • •

December 29, 1989

The day was so perfect, the new mother thinks, as a tear of joy trickles from her tired eyes. She can't help but think, it seems too perfect; it must be a dream!

Her fingers tighten up a little as she shakes him a little to see if he is okay. *Something is not right,* she thinks. His chest isn't moving, and she wonders why he is holding his breath. Then the realization hits her. His face is a shade of blue, as if his skin is a reflection of his bedroom wall color, but there is a shocking quality to the color. Then, again, it hits her . . .

"NOOOOOOOOOOOOOOOOOOO!"

Once the echo hits his eardrums, the toolbox drops out of his grasp, and his feet start moving like the pace of sticks beating rapidly on drums. He runs up the wooden staircase, then stands by helplessly as he sees that his wife has moved into automatic mode from her nurse's training, and has begun CPR. Pushing back the panic, she desperately tries to reverse the trauma. She yells at her husband, telling him, "Call 911! Call 911!" He realizes this is a situation he cannot fix. He dials 911.

When the paramedics arrive, her pale cheeks are covered in tears. When the husband sees his distraught wife, he wants nothing more than to be able to fix this. But he hasn't been able to help. Relieved of her duties, the mother drops to her knees, and she holds her husband's legs, sobbing. She looks down on her stunning diamond and sapphire necklace and wishes she could go back to four days ago.

The pained couple waits by the silent crib. There is no sound of cooing, laughter, or crying. The baby blue room sits in the shadow of the big oak tree that is just outside the windowsill. The room takes on a cold, dark aura, and is no longer cheerful. The baby is not alive; the room no longer houses Austin in this life.

It is now the room that Austin had once lived in; it was his temporary home.

• • • •

Although that day was tragic for young Austin's family, when his parents knew he was not coming back, they made a magnanimous, lifesaving decision to help others. They chose to donate Austin's organs. Fortunately, I was the recipient of his heart (which is still with me today). I recognize the difficult decision his mother and father were faced with, and cannot express my gratitude enough to them for their selfless act. It is truly a miracle that people whom I never knew, and who never knew I existed, were willing to do that, so that I could be here today to write my story. Austin and his family have taught me a very important virtue: every day is a gift. I'm able to tell you my story because of Austin's family, who, despite their great loss, were able to give a gift that will last me my entire life.

I've always imagined that incident occurred right before or quickly after my parents were faced with a difficult realization: my life expectancy was three days. My parents, sleeping after a fitful night, awoke to a musical alarm. It was very loud—almost distorted. Mom was angry, thinking Dad had set an alarm clock that was disturbing the first bit of sleep she'd had in days. In fact, the radio played spontaneously. No one had set the alarm. On its own, the radio began to play a hit by B. J. Thomas called "I Just Can't Help Believing."

With the words "This time the girl is gonna stay," Dad said, "The song: It's an OMEN!"

Mom and Dad stayed at Grandma's (Dad's mom). It was closer to the hospital than was their own home, and it provided a break from the intensity of the last few days. It was a familiar place to have a private shower and get recharged for more of the vigil.

The bright sun filled the cold room. Moisture collecting on the window blurred the view but confirmed that the cold spell continued. The upstairs bedroom had never had heat. Grandma thought the heat rising from the kitchen below was enough. The warm feather comforter invited my parents to stay tucked in, but the music, though peaceful, was urgent.

It was peaceful but crisp outside on this frigid December Sunday morning. Soon everyone would be heading down the block in front of the house; my Grandma called all the traffic the Dutch 500—the street to the Dutch Reformed Church.

The smell of coffee drifted upstairs. While he was up and ready to begin the day, she lingered, not quite ready to face what could be the last day.

She turned toward the window. Just at that moment, an orange tree—brought from Grandpa's office and positioned in the bright sun, in the warmest spot of the room—dropped its sole fruit. This act, along with the radio song, seemed an eerie coincidence. With Grandpa's death two months earlier, the family longed for his presence. Grandpa's untimely death, his unnecessary death, his absence created a void, especially apparent now when some wisdom was needed. On his favorite office plant, there lingered one lonely orange from the time when he was alive. It was difficult to grasp. He had watched the tree blossom, he was alive to see the flower unfold and the fruit form, but was not alive to see the fruit mature. Grandpa's last orange. The fruit had matured since Grandpa's death just two months earlier. It chose this moment to ripen to the point it could detach from branch where it had held on for the growing season. Plop. It bounced from the table to the floor next to the bed where she watched, stunned.

They arose with renewed energy and awe, ready to face this day, because they believed that their baby girl would be all right.

4
Anastasia Claire
"The Prayer" by Celine Dion and Andrea Bocelli

Some basic facts about December 22, 1989:
- It is the 356th day of the year.
- It is only nine days until the end of the year.
- It is Indonesian Mother's Day.
- It is the date of the Spanish Christmas Lottery.
- It is the birth date of Logan Huffman, an American actor who has appeared in the 2009 remake of "V". (He's cute!)
- It is also the birth date of "American Idol" winner Jordan Sparks.

An unpleasant fact connected with the number 22: My Aunt Carol passed away at the age of 22, due to leukemia.

About the 25th:
- My Grandpa Aggen died October 25, 1989.
- My great aunt passed away November 25, 1989.
- I was born December 22nd, and it was predicted I would live three days. December 25th could have been my heavenly birthday. Three months in a row, three deaths.

• • • •

It's no surprise that the 22nd day of each month brings me both joy and sadness. My birth was a day of mixed emotions too. My parents have shared recollections of the time I was born.

Passing empty cornfields, dormant for the winter and covered by an icy blanket of white, it was the coldest night on record for this date. They always refer to the field in a really cold football game as frozen tundra. I know this because my dad is a football coach, but, from what everyone tells me, December 22, 1989, was true tundra—the kind of tundra where wind swirls and blows drifts of snow. I always envision there would have been some wolves, howling on a mountaintop, but that's my active imagination. It was 21 degrees below zero Fahrenheit when my parents drove the ten miles to the hospital. It was a night filled with anticipation. My brother rested with grandparents, who were waiting anxiously to relay the good news in the next few hours.

The nurses told my Dad what a wonderful coach he was through my mother's labor. This coaching required much different techniques than what he uses with his football players. My mother isn't the screaming type, and against everyone's directions she closed her eyes, pushed, and I was born.

IT'S A GIRL!
Name: Anastasia Claire Aggen
Date of Birth: December 22, 1989
Time of Birth: 3:47 a.m.
Weight: 7 lbs., 13 ounces
Height: 21 inches
Parents: Dave and Janet Aggen
All is well.

5
A New Heart for Christmas
"All I Want for Christmas" by Mariah Carey

I am wrapped safely in the comfort of my mother's arms. My eyes are closed, shutting out the unfamiliar white lights, in the pastel birthing room. Slowly, my lips turn blue and my skin fades, the flesh tone turning an iridescent, ghostly white.

A nurse places her stethoscope against my chest and then quickly whisks me out of my safety zone as my stunned parents watch helplessly. Though dangerously short of breath, I scream and cry for my mother. I am put into a sterile, impersonal incubator like the baby chicks at the museum, waiting to hatch. Newly born, I am unaware of my inability to breathe on my own. Soon my organs will shut down. A clear mask is placed firmly over my tiny nose and mouth. It covers most of my face, while the pediatricians who have just met me begin hand ventilation that will continue for six hours, until I am transported to another new, "special" place. The electric ventilator has not been invented. My new life begins with pushing and pressure against my chest every few seconds.

Many hands poke me, and I sense their prodding, as my skin is squeezed in the location of various organs. I am having a hard time gasping for air. The doctor enters the room where I was delivered to consult. More diagnosis will be needed at a skilled center, and I will be transferred shortly.

It is just three days until Christmas—the most wonderful time of the year, the happiest season of all. **Not this year. Not for me**. I am too little to know better—and of course I don't remember any of this now. My parents can fill in the blanks, as they have through the years retold to me how so many people came together to help through a very difficult period. All of this could not be told without the miracle provided by Austin's gift.

• • • •

My six-year-old brother went to school on the day I was born. He was in second grade. It was the last day of school before his winter break started! This particular Friday was a very special day. He walked into his second-grade classroom with a huge smile on his face. He swelled with pride because now he was a big brother. Our grandparents had told him the news that morning. Now Dave tells me he was looking forward to a new playmate but would miss calling me "Beulah," which was his name for me while I was in the womb.

"Okay class," the teacher called. "Please sit down, and sit quietly. The bell rang."

Dave walked to his desk politely, with his shoulders arched back, strong and proud as if he was a superhero. He felt like this was one of the best days of his life.

"Today we are going to do an art project that you will have time to finish. You will be able to take it home to show your family! Since winter break begins tomorrow, we are going to make a drawing of what you look forward to doing during the holiday! This afternoon we will have our holiday party."

Dave was anxious for class to be over.

"What are you going to draw, Dave?" asked his classmate, Lauren.

"Christmas with my family. What are you going to draw, Lauren?"

"I'm going to draw the pony I want for Christmas. You can use my markers if you want. I'll share with you."

Dave was impressed and thought Lauren, with her long brown hair and cute smile, was really nice to offer to share her markers with him.

"Okay. Sure. Thanks, Lauren."

They smiled at each other, and went on with drawing.

The day passed quickly, and the school bell rang at last rang. It was officially time to get ready to go home and begin vacation. There was so much anticipation at this moment. No school for two whole weeks! Family parties. Two whole weeks of vacation, and Mom would be home with his new sister. Dad would be off work, too. Maybe there'd be some time for sledding, snowmen, skating, or ice fishing. Maybe the G.I. Joe Space Center would be under the tree, his dream of dreams because it involved astronauts and manliness. It would be a *huge* box. Dave packed his backpack and grabbed his lunch box as fast as he could. He put on his warmly lined navy blue jacket and ran out of classroom. Grandpa's white Crown Victoria with the blue velvet seats would be waiting for him. Years later, when Grandpa stopped driving, that 1985 rear-wheel drive tank, so full of memories, would become Brother Dave's first car. The velvety interior won him many compliments. He smiled at Grandpa, and jumped in the white wonder-mobile.

Climbing into the back seat, his joy was snatched away when, in a gentle voice, Grandpa spoke. "Your new baby sister is having some trouble. She has to go to a special hospital. Would you like to go see her before she goes?"

"*Yes!* Let's hurry! Will she be okay, Grandpa?" he asked as he fastened his seat belt.

"Everyone is taking very good care of her, but we better hurry. She is getting her first helicopter ride today. She will be going to the Children's Hospital."

Grandma sat in the passenger seat. Grandma's strength was her ability to find the positive in any situation, or to find the good in every person. She used to tell us, when we have a disagreement with someone, to "go over the mountain of kindness," which to this day is still a great rule to live by. Surprisingly, Grandma didn't add any good news. Even she was having trouble finding something encouraging to say. She kept searching; sure enough, she came up with, "Isn't it something that your sister was born on the coldest day of the year, 21 below zero?"

"A helicopter ride! How cool is that! I am six years old, and I haven't even been in one yet," said Dave.

Soon, Grandma added, "She is a Friday child, Dave, loving and giving."

"Grandma, what day of the week was I born?" asked Dave.

Grandma answered, "Thursday, Dave. You have far to go. " She had a remarkable memory.

By the time they arrived in Barrington, Illinois, the incubator and its precious cargo were headed to the helicopter pad. Reverend Gary Miller, our church pastor at the time, grabbed Dave's hand and rushed to help him get a glimpse of me, his baby sister. Having served on the town's volunteer ambulance team, he was familiar with the emergency corridors, and holding Dave's hand, Rev. Gary guided Dave through a maze of corridors not intended for small children, past the disapproving staff, and out to the helicopter port, where he got his glimpse and formed the memory that he *had* a sister.

Ignoring the unusual circumstances of meeting the newborn, ignoring the machines, tubes, and personnel that surrounded her, Dave only saw a glimpse of me. Dave tells me Reverend Miller pleaded with the helicopter pilot to let Dave see me. Unaware of the argument that had just taken place between the minister and hospital doctors regarding whether or not Dave should or should not see me, six-year-old Dave was not too impressed by the tightly wrapped baby whose eyes were closed. Encased in the Plexiglas box, she did remind him of Snow White. The doctors felt seeing his sister in this state would be a traumatic memory. Rev. Gary felt the point was that he *would have* a memory, and strongly voiced his opinion that that was a most important consideration.

It was time to travel the 35 miles to the Children's Hospital in Chicago, Illinois, which by helicopter would be approximately twelve minutes. The precious cargo *(me)* was now en route; there was nothing else to do at this hospital, so Dave went home with Grandpa and Grandma to put the finishing touches on Grandma's annual gingerbread masterpiece and to dream of the G.I. Joe Space Center that was at the top of his Christmas list. The dreams of astronauts diverted his concerns that his younger sibling would be riding in a helicopter before he had such an opportunity.

Later, like most children, I asked Mom to tell me about the day I was born. She often gave a heavy sigh. "What part do you want to me to tell you? How much time do you have?" she asked.

"Tell me about how I got to the Children's Hospital," I often suggested.

"You left in the helicopter. We had waited hours for an ambulance, but they kept going to get children who they felt were in worse shape than you. We felt lucky that you were better; we were relieved that they were going to get other children, because that meant you weren't in dire shape. It led us to be a little hopeful. But as the hours wore on, you weren't getting better, and we thought of more questions. We were getting anxious to find out what you needed, what was wrong. We hoped you would be with the whole family for your first Christmas.

"After you left, there was a lot of confusion in the hospital. I wanted to be released to go to be with you. Aunt Donna began to bag my belongings, hurrying me on my way. I didn't know that Rev. Gary had conferred with her, and told Donna it was urgent that I get to Chicago."

My mom continues telling me more. . . .

"While we got ready, Rev. Gary usurped a van from his secretary (and my friend, whom I called Beautiful Betty), and drove us down the Kennedy Expressway like a professional stock car driver. Betty and I were in the back seat of the van, and the windows were fogging up because it was so cold. The back seat of a van isn't the best place to be sitting right after you have a baby, and the bouncing had me laughing and crying at the same time. Though our trip was longer than the 12 minutes your helicopter ride took, time seemed suspended.

"There was a glitch. Betty's daughters, Sarah and Liz, had brought the van to the hospital because Betty came with Gary in his car, which wasn't large enough for all of us. The girls would take Gary's car back to Algonquin. It was very dark and cold, and Liz was a new driver. No one had cell phones or a GPS. After we left Barrington, Dad, always a voice of reason, expressed his concern that Betty's girls got home safely. He made Gary pull into a gas station to call their home to make sure they had arrived safely. But there was no answer. Dad couldn't stand the idea that they were lost in a dark, cold cornfield, and he *insisted* we go looking for them. When we finally connected, the girls were a little panicky. This was understandable given the situation. The area around the hospital was undeveloped—no houses, no streetlights, no gas stations. The girls didn't know which direction they were driving. There was no moonlight. We gave them directions on how we thought they could get home. But they were still lost. They finally found civilization, much to all our relief, and then we could resume our journey. I think this pushed Gary to drive faster. I don't know whether he thought about what he would tell the police if we were stopped, but, amazingly, we were not. You know, Dad wouldn't drive above the speed limit, but he didn't say a thing; he concentrated on what needed to happen when we got to the new hospital.

"Contrasted with the whirlwind of activity that surrounded the first hours after your birth—with the information and decisions that were needed to prepare for the 'rapid' departure from hospital number one—the quiet lobby of hospital number two was deserted. There were a couple of plain Christmas trees with only a few twinkling lights. No staff, no visitors, no activity. In 1989, there were no security guards to greet you at the door of the hospital. The staff had left to prepare for their holidays, and the hospital was operating with a skeleton crew. No one sat at the welcome desk to direct us. Having given birth just hours earlier, I asked Dad to find a wheelchair; I was feeling a little weak and didn't know how long it would take to find you. Dad searched for a wheelchair, and we looked around the lobby trying to figure out where to go. When Dad came back with the wheelchair, I was grateful to sit down. The fit was a little tight, and it didn't occur at that moment that the tight fit of the wheelchair seat was due to the fact it was meant for children, not for a post-delivery bloated woman. Gary and Betty found personnel who directed us to a conference room on the 9th floor. A co-coordinator appeared, and we were escorted to a meeting room, where several doctors introduced themselves and gave their *diagnosis*. I was very anxious to get to see you! What was happening to you, I wondered; I didn't want you to be alone. By the amount of information the team was sharing, it was evident that you had been through a lot. Each new face, each nameless doctor rattled off his or her impressions, and one seemed less hopeful than the next. I wanted to leave, because this information wasn't helping, but I didn't know where you were. *Finally*, the new chief of surgery was introduced. It was his first day as the boss. He didn't know where you were either! But he finally summed up all the observation and concluded that it was unlikely you would live more than three days. Until December 25th: Christmas.

"As we prepared to go to see you, one doctor mentioned that you could be listed for a heart transplant. Generally, the wait was three months, and, because you had a three-day window, chances were unlikely that a heart would be available."

Mom continued, "The neo-natal intensive care unit team of specialists concluded that your heart would not support your life because of atrial and mitral valve stenosis. With this heart defect, you *might* live three days. You needed a miracle, and you needed it fast. Without a new heart you might never have had a chance to experience Christmas."

"Someone asked, 'Would you like to see your daughter?' As we walked down the hall, we were surprised to see Grandma Aggen, Uncle Jim, Aunt Nene, Uncle George, Aunt Kathy B., Uncle Dan, and Aunt Kathy. I wasn't aware that they had been called. But you know how nutty our family is about babies! I felt silly in the kids' wheelchair, but not strong enough to get up and give everyone a hug, and I wanted to go see you!

"Finally we were guided to the NICU—the neo-natal intensive care unit. Babies in the area could only come in as newborns if they came straight from the hospital where they were born. Babies who had gone home and needed to return were sent to PICU—the pediatric intensive care unit. We met the neonatologist, Dr. Collins, who was upbeat in spite of all the challenges surrounding him. We were getting closer to finding you, but first we were introduced to isolation preparation. We had to wear gowns, masks, and booties over our shoes like the ones they give you at house walks, wash our hands, put on sterile gloves, and then enter the unit. Dr. Collins led us to you, explaining that, to conserve the little strength left in your heart, they had put you in a coma-like state. He told us that you could hear us, feel if we touched you, but that you could not respond because of the *Pavulon*. We were shocked that most of the hair on your hair had been shaved so that tubes could be inserted into your head; and there were tubes or lines as they called them into your tiny feet. Dr. Collins told us that the IV would supply nutrition and all the medication you needed. All you were wearing was a diaper, and I worried you were uncomfortable, cold, or in pain. Dr. Collins assured us that you were not feeling pain, and that you were comfortable because all the monitors gave them information about your vitals. Soon we would learn what each vital meant—your respirations, blood pressure, and blood oxygen levels. Soon we would compare the numbers that told whether your organs were failing, inching you farther away from life in this world.

"After our first visit, we had to sign many forms, and go to the admission office. I knew very little about insurance, but felt grateful that we were covered because both Dad and I worked and had insurance.

"Signing all the forms, the name Anastasia was a bit cumbersome. I suggested to Dad that we should reconsider because it took too long to fill in the blanks. Then, I realized no one had asked us about information for your birth certificate. There was so much to be done, and I wanted to go back and watch the monitor that showed you were breathing. I wanted to be sure the oxygen saturation stayed above 92 so that you wouldn't have brain damage.

"Grandma Aggen suggested her own name, 'Helen,' would be perfect.

"I always liked 'Claire.' Dad liked 'Katie.'

"We called home to say good night to Dave, who was staying with Grandpa and Grandma in Lake in the Hills. 'Hi, Mom,' Dave said. 'Tell Dad that *she looks just like Lauren in my class.* I hope I see you soon. 'Night, Mom. Love you!'

"Dad and I continued our discussion about finding a short name for you, since Anastasia was too long of a name for medical paper work. We thought about how the other member of the family, your brother, thought you looked like a Lauren. And that's how you were named 'Lauren Ann.'

"Uncle George was anxious to see you. He held back his tears as he gowned up, so disappointed he couldn't hug you. He is a sucker for babies, always has been, and can't stay away from them. Uncle George was stunned as he slowly entered and was faced by a tiny baby dwarfed by all the medical apparatus.

"'She's so still,' he whispered.

"'They've given her a drug to conserve her strength,' I said to Uncle George. 'She can hear and feel, but she can't respond. I think it's awful—how can they be sure she isn't in pain?' I asked.

"'Aunt Kathy B.'s turn next; she held back trying to play with your hair and straighten the bow, being the hairdresser she is. The eternal optimist, she hugged me and said, 'I just feel it. She'll be fine! Lauren will be pulling the Tupperware out of your cabinets in no time.'

"Grandma Aggen had been through a lot, with Grandpa's death two months earlier. She couldn't bear to spend Thanksgiving without Grandpa; she volunteered at a food kitchen instead of spending the day with us, because she wouldn't have been able to stop crying. She tried to hold back the tears and almost fell down when she walked into the room. Choking back the tears, she hoarsely whimpered, 'Dad was so excited about this baby. He could hardly wait for her to be born.'

"Visiting hours in NICU never end. The only time parents aren't allowed was the hour during shift changes when records were updated and nurses briefed their replacements. It was the beginning of charting on computers. Record keeping took hours, because the staff had to fill in the necessary information longhand on paper and then transfer it into the new computer system. But the paper chart at the foot of your bed had all the numbers. Kidneys better or worse, oxygen sufficient or not, respirations slow or fast, heartbeats . . . regular, tachycardia, bradycardia, arrhythmia, EKG, EEG, ECHO . . . and on and on. But one doctor told us, 'Look at her. Numbers don't tell it all.'

"Amid all the beeps of the monitors, and the quiet—the absence of newborn crying—there were moments to think. Are you really comfortable? How long will you be in this state? Can you die even, hooked up to all these machines? Someone else's baby has to die for you to live. You can't get a part of a heart from a living donor. After another baby dies, you might get a chance to live. If you match. If it is in time. Three days. What happens to make a baby die but doesn't damage the heart? Car accident. Gunshot. A baby is born with a defect that won't allow him or her to survive—how can that heart sustain you?

"One friend at Church had just lost a baby boy who died from swallowing merconium during birth. She was kind enough to talk to me about the arrangements they made for their son.

"'It provides people with a place to start talking to you,' she said. 'The service was so nice, or I'm sorry we couldn't get to the service because we were out of town.'

"Dad and I knew we had to make plans. We were comforted when we found out that you could be buried above Grandpa Aggen. Reverend Gary brought a wonderful book intended to explain death to children. He suggested I read it to begin a conversation with Dave to help him understand death. It helped me. *Water Bugs and Dragonflies* told the story of bug friends who changed. When the dragonfly bounced through the surface of the water, he couldn't go back. He was in a new body, and realized his friends wouldn't recognize him if he did go back. He had to wait until they changed, and then they'd understand what happened. And then the dragonfly went on to explore in his new and wonderful world.

"Then we remembered, you had not been baptized! So we sent Betty went to look for Reverend Gary. He came in, and right in NICU, you were baptized Lauren Ann Aggen.

"That was a lot for your first day of life!"

· · · ·

"Then it was Day 2," my mom said. "You were hanging on. Dave drew a picture to hang above your bassinette. Some volunteer ladies made tiny pink baby booties for you. Knowledgeable about isolation practices, they sealed them in a zip lock bag so no germs came into your room. However, they were huge when we put them on your feet! Another volunteer brought you your first teddy bear. It had pink rosebuds around its head. We sang Christmas carols on that Saturday while everyone else was hustling and bustling with their holiday happenings.

"On Day 3, the insurance company called.

"'We feel this treatment is experimental,' they said. 'We recommend you take your baby home and let nature take its course. We are no longer responsible for any medical expenses.'

"A nurse told me there was a call for me."

"'Mrs. Aggen,' the voice said, 'this is the business office. Please come down to fill in some paperwork.'

"When I got to the office, a woman informed me, 'Mrs. Aggen, you owe $78,000 for today's services. Your insurance company is not covering anything; they are declining treatment. How much can you pay today?'

"'I don't have my purse with me,' I said. 'I'll go upstairs to get it.'"

Mom left, but she never went back. Family friends Tim and Karen Bondy came for support. Mom told me, "Tim said, 'Worry about your baby now. There will be time to worry about the money later.'

"Each person coming to wish you a Merry Christmas took a turn as they visited, two by two, wearing scrubs, masks, and gloves, to wish you . . . a miracle. It was a very long day, watching you. You never moved or made any sounds. There were bright lights in the unit, and the sounds of machines whirring, beeping, or buzzing. There were other critically ill babies sharing the room, with one nurse for each baby. Dave brought you a Minnie Mouse mobile that usually hangs over cribs, but here it was hanging from an IV pole, playing soft music. Dave looked cute in his yellow gown. One of the nurses drew a smiley face on his mask! The irony looking back is that we knew you couldn't see in your induced coma state, but we thought you could hear. Perhaps you could, maybe the drugs hadn't killed your auditory nerves yet. We kept watching you breathe, watching the numbers, encouraging you to breathe when they got low or slow. Merry Christmas!"

• • • •

The story continued: "On Day 4, I was sick. I felt awful. I didn't want to enter NICU for fear of passing germs. I decided to go home and go to the emergency room. The young intern asked, 'What brings you to the emergency room when you could be at the after-Christmas sales?'

"I told my problems to the ER doctor: 'I just gave birth, I'm in pain and have a cough. I feel awful. I gave birth a few days ago, and my baby is dying. I want to get well so I can spend time with her—as much time as she has.'

"He told me I had bronchitis. 'After 24 hours on antibiotics, it will be safe for you to return to the hospital. Would you like something to help you sleep? Do you want something to ease your anguish?'

Mom told him she needed to stay alert to keep track of what was happening. So she took the antibiotics. Dad stayed with me.

"When I got back home," Mom continued, "Grandma Aggen had fixed her special barbecued ribs. They were delicious! Now, that's *your* favorite meal. It was difficult to eat during those long days. On the other hand, it was during this week that we met and began a twenty-year relationship with the famous chef 'Bettye.' She held the honor of being the employee who had been there the longest. With the sweetest voice, and the kindest manner, she brightened the day of so many families. You couldn't help but feel encouraged after just a few words with her. Her delicious pancakes and grilled-to-order breakfasts were a highlight every morning in the basement cafeteria. She always had a smile, asked about the children, remembered who was who, and always kept everyone in her prayers. When she retires, the hospital will need a lot more social workers! She was an angel!"

"Day 5," Mom said, "you were holding on. You were number one on the national waiting list.

"By Day 6," she said, "it was starting to wear on me. Even when I tried, I couldn't sleep well. I spent each night on couches in the hospital hall, or in the lounge. The hospital provided sheets and a pillow. Dad went home at night to spend some time with Dave. I asked about feeding you breast milk. No one really answered, but I pumped and froze milk in little bottles. If they could feed you formula, I thought, why couldn't they feed you breast milk? I believed it would be good for your immunity and your brain development to have my breast milk. Little neurons keep making connections when babies get breast milk. You needed all the help you could get. There was no private place to pump milk. I locked myself in a little closet every few hours, trying to keep the milk going for the time when you could drink it. I was too naive to realize I was talking with pediatric specialists, not women's health specialists who could advise *me*.

"By the afternoon of Day 7," Mom continued, "your heart rate and oxygen saturation were dropping. For seven days I had watched you lie motionless as you were poked and prodded, stuck and drugged. I didn't know how long you could stand this—I didn't know how long *I* could stand it. We met with the team; they felt your condition was worsening. There was a machine that could help, they told us. It had been used successfully on adults, but never children. They were trying to locate an ECMO, short for extracorporeal membrane oxygenation, and someone to run it. 'It could give her more time,' they said.

"Late in the afternoon, they had located the ECMO. However, the hospital declined its use, saying it was an unknown with babies, and no profusionist was trained to use it with a baby.

"By early evening, the doctor who had experience at his former hospital offered to stay all night and run the machine. The hospital refused. This was a wild roller coaster ride."

That night, doctors told my parents that it was amazing how long I had stuck it out, but time was running out.

"It was likely," Mom continued, "that night, your one week birthday, would be your last. The next day, they would have to remove your name from the waiting list; you had become too ill to survive surgery.

"I was exhausted and decided to go home for a shower and a nap. I wanted to be ready for the next day. As I put on my coat, a nurse asked where I was going. I explained that I wanted to go home and have a shower.

"The staff nurse hesitated, but then spoke softly. 'Unofficially, I think you might want to be staying a bit longer. We have a possibility. We are checking because we think we have a match.'

"With the shortage of organs, it is the sickest patient who receives an available organ. You were the sickest baby at that point."

. . . .

My father told me the story of the night I got a new heart.

"The transplant coordinator received a call about a possible match from a three-month-old baby boy in Austin, Texas."

He died from SIDS; it was surprising that a heart that didn't work for that baby could work for me.

"One concern of UNOS (the United Network for Organ Sharing)," Dad told me, "was whether the surgeon from Chicago could fly to Texas, recover the heart, and return within five hours. Five hours is the limit that the walnut-sized organ could be outside the body without becoming damaged. The Children's Doctor headed to Texas, keeping in contact with the Chicago team."

As my Dad said, "Lauren, you were *very* sick. The doctors decided to go ahead; there was no turning back. Your status was deteriorating quickly. In fact, the team had talked to Mom and me about removing your name from the transplant waiting list. You were getting too sick to survive the transplant surgery. After the decision was made to send a doctor to Texas, there was no turning back. But each few minutes, their concern about you surviving the next few hours was growing.

"The surgeon came to speak with us: 'We need to conserve what strength her body has left. We think the best option is to begin to use the heart lung machine. Lauren's heart will be removed while the donor heart is in transit. Once the recovery team leaves Texas, we will begin surgery here. There will be no second choice. If the new heart isn't in healthy condition, there will be no alternative.'

"The recovery team left Chicago, carrying a red and white igloo cooler, in a Learjet. That small container would carry your new heart back to the Chicago surgery room. It was about 10 p.m. when they left."

My Dad continued to tell about that night: "After some arrangements were made, the transplant co-coordinator came with the surgeon to speak to us. He said, 'The neonatal intensive care unit is on the ninth floor. The surgical unit is on the second floor. In Lauren's weakened state, the pressure changes in the elevator ride could be devastating. We are going to have to transport her, with all the equipment, down the stairwell. A team will move her incubator down seven floors, step by step, allowing her body to adjust to the changes. With the gradual adjustment, we hope she will survive the trip down to the second floor.'

"We watched the team begin the descent, and then took the elevator down to the second floor to wait. It took more than an hour to complete the trip. You were hanging on, barely. I kissed your forehead, and then you were pushed through the double doors to prepare for surgery. The next time we saw you, you would have a new heart from a donor.

"A nurse came out to tell us she would be the liaison between the surgical unit to keep us informed about the progress. It seemed she also kept us aware of the complications that were arising. Once you were safely on the heart lung machine, we felt more confident that you would survive the next hours until the heart arrived.

"Then the nurse relayed the message that the donor heart had passed the required tests. 'What kind of tests?' we asked.

"There were criteria that were important to the success of the operation. If there were anatomical problems, unexpected diseases, or infections, the transplant would be cancelled.

"The donor heart passed all the criteria; another bullet had been dodged. Now the team would hop back into the Learjet to return to Chicago. The flight was expected to arrive in the early morning hours. This is the time of day that most transplants occur. The large surgical waiting room had couches, where many of the family stretched out for the long wait. The blue-vinyl-clad, armless, low-seating chairs also could be pushed together to allow enough room to lie down. There were several people keeping vigil with us. During the day, the chairs and couches would be filled with families waiting while tubes were inserted in ears, corrective heart procedures were completed, and orthopedic surgeries as well as a variety of other problems were addressed. This night, members of our family and friends were the only people in the surgical waiting room on the second floor. Outside, the tiny lights twinkled on the parkway trees beside a very quiet Halsted Street, void of any vehicular traffic. The normally busy Lincoln Park bars had closed, and there were no pedestrians on the typically busy side streets.

"The nurse returned, saying, 'The plane is en route, and Lauren is stable for the time being.'"

• • • •

Dad continued the story, telling of December 30, 1989. "The large picture windows in the waiting room were getting frosty. The frigid air outside contrasted with the inside temperatures," my Dad recalled. "Steam rising from the sewers and manholes looked peculiar, as if things were upside down, coming out instead of going in.

"About 1:30 a.m., the nurse returned and sat down. 'We have a problem,' she grimly reported. 'O'Hare has just closed due to icy conditions. The jet carrying the heart cannot land here. Alternates are being considered, but the other airports are closing. Airports more than an hour drive from here can't be used because a donated organ cannot survive outside the body for more than five hours. Things don't look good. We haven't given up, but we are running out of solutions, and time.'

"The heart lung machine was doing its job, but there wasn't much time left. The road conditions were becoming treacherous due to the icy conditions. Shortly, we learned that the jet would be landing in Milwaukee. However, that was more than a one-hour drive, and the drive would be too long to get the heart to the surgical unit in time. Once off the plane, the recovery team entered the airport trying to find a solution. They could not drive to Chicago fast enough, especially with the poor road conditions.

As the surgeon was communicating with the Chicago surgical unit from an airport phone, a pilot walking nearby saw the cooler labeled 'human organ' and overheard the conversation. 'Excuse me, Doctor,' the pilot interrupted. 'Does the hospital have a helicopter pad?'

"'Yes.'

"The pilot said, 'I have a helicopter outside, and, with clearance, I can have your team and the heart in Chicago in a half hour.'

"Shortly after, lights on the roof were turned on, and the copter blades' sounds increased as the precious cargo approached. A few minutes later, still wearing warm coats, the team rushed past the waiting room door carrying the cooler. As they entered the surgical unit, we heard a loud cheer from the staff. I got goose bumps then, and I still do now when I remember that moment.

"The nurse came back to say the surgery had begun, and in about two hours you would be in recovery—and by morning you would be in ICU. We were exhausted and marveled that the surgeons could be completing their miraculous efforts in the wee early hours of the morning after a full day of work.

"I don't remember the other updates, but after just about an hour the surgeons came out to tell us things were looking promising. 'In fact,' said the surgeon, 'we normally use the paddles to start the heart. Once in place, this heart just started beating on its own.'

"We had to pause and marvel; a heart so small, the size of a walnut, started to beat on its own. We said a prayer for your donor's family, whose tragedy could not be averted.

"In the early morning hours, while it was still dark outside, we were taken to see the room where you would recover, and taught some of the rules that would be important to the success of your healing.

"Your personal, special nurses—Julia and Lauren—who would be keeping special watch over you, began teaching us: 'Lauren will be in an isolation room. There is a special entrance with a hallway area that has a negative airflow to help control infection. Every time you enter this hallway, you will scrub your hands, wear a mask, gloves, gown and booties. Avoid bringing in germs! Anything that enters the main room must be sterile. No plush animals, knit blankets; only items that are sterile, washed at home, brought in plastic bags that could be discarded in the hallway will be allowed into the room.'

"Very quickly we had switched from waiting to a frenzy of preparation. Everyone was anxious for you to be in your special room recovering.

"Julie and Lauren began to explain the medications regime that would help your body accept your new heart. Just then the surgeon stopped in. 'Things are looking good,' he said. 'Now we have to watch and wait for signs of rejection.'

"He paused, then said, 'They all reject. We have to catch it, but it is treatable.'

"We hadn't processed that word, 'rejection.' We understood that you had exchanged a life-ending condition for a chronic condition. You would take anti-rejection medications for as long as you had your transplant. That meant forever. The drugs, the immunosuppressives, would make you more vulnerable to illness. They had side affects; they could damage your kidneys. They could cause cancer. They could make you hairy. I don't think we dwelled on these, because we were so grateful for the miracle that you were alive. We were so grateful to your donor family."

• • • •

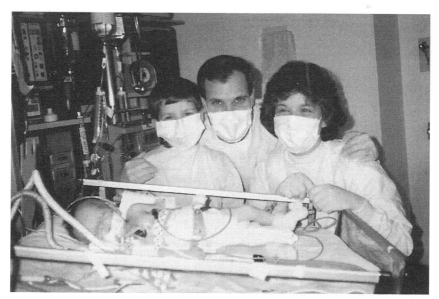

Picture in ICU after receiving my new heart, as my family stayed by my side.
From left: Dave, Dad, and Mom—and me with all the tubes, of course.

Dear Lauren,

It was the Saturday between Christmas and New Years when we had planned our open house for friends and family. Of course your parents were on the guest list too! The invitations were sent, the house was cleaned, our decorations had been up since Thanksgiving, and all the hors d'oeuvres were made and waiting for our guests. I had baked my usual assortment of Christmas cookies, which were waiting to be devoured! I think I even made two of your favorites, the meringues and chocolate-covered cherries, that year too! People arrived, drinks and snacks were served, and the party was in full swing! During the evening your dad called and said, "We have a heart." My own heart almost stopped because the call came unexpectedly, and I got so excited. When I returned to the family room and announced this great news, everyone just got quiet. Some tears were shed too! When people found out that donors were needed to see if their blood would be a match for you, folks started deciding who would go to the hospital and who would stay to continue "partying." Naturally everyone was a little bit "hyper," and moving cars in the driveway was in order. Unfortunately, we'd had some ice build up on the front stairs, and my sister, Dorothy, fell going out to move her car. She was wearing heels and tells me she has not worn them since that night. Her tailbone was sore for quite a while after her spill!

The details of who went with whom in what vehicle are lost to me now. However, I do remember that John Novak drove several people in his van. Those I remember were the late Ward Edwards, Pam Novak, Rich and Debbie Strout, and me. There may have been more, but I just don't remember! Roger stayed at home with the remaining guests. I think they had a good time . . . at least I hope so!!

So, my dear, you definitely were the center of attention that night! Over the years we have had other holiday parties, but none was as spectacular as that Saturday night in 1989!

Love,
Beautiful Betty

6
A+

"The Reason" by Hoobastank

Did you know that every three seconds someone needs blood? The day I received my heart, I needed blood, and, according to the stories I have heard growing up, it wasn't easy finding a CMV negative, A positive blood donor, after 10:00 p.m., New Year's weekend.

• • • •

My future godmother, Beautiful Betty, was having a Christmas party on December 30, 1989. My parents belong to the Congregational Church of Algonquin, where they became good friends with Betty and Roger Paldauf. That night, Betty and Roger were having a holiday gathering. Those attending did not expect the interruption that began with the phone ringing.

"Hello?" Betty answered as she cupped one hand over her ear. She stood so tall and confident, eager to get this phone conversation over with so she could go back to hosting her party. She glanced at the crowd that appeared to be a blur of red and green as she tried to comprehend the message. While the ladies were enjoying sampling the treats, the men were talking about sports and business. Betty swiftly lowered her shoulders; the longer she held the phone, the more worried became her look.

Blood types

A, B, AB, O. Rh positive or negative.

I needed live blood donors that were both A positive and CMV negative.

My family couldn't donate blood because they were CMV positive. Only Chris, the son of one couple from the party, and Uncle George's minister were negative. Chris was negative because he was young and hadn't been exposed to CMV. Uncle George's minister was from Minnesota, where it is colder than in our part of the Midwest. People who live in colder climates are generally less likely to be exposed to CMV. *It's crazy to think that, out of all the people who came to get tested to see if they could give me blood (more than 50 people), only two could match the type of blood I needed. A positive was easy to find, but not CMV negative. Fortunately, some hospital employees were matches and also helped out by donating that night!*

About Cytomegalovirus

Cytomegalovirus (CMV) is a common virus that most people get sometime during their life. It is a virus that is carried by people, not associated with water, food, or animals. It is in the herpes virus family, and similar to other viruses like Epstein Barr and mononucleosis. It can become dormant for a while and may activate at a later time. It is spread from person to person by direct contact. It is shed in urine, saliva, and semen and can be passed through blood transfusion or organ transplantation. An infected mother can give it to her fetus or newborn.

Many people do not have symptoms when they get CMV. Those who do have symptoms complain of fever, swollen glands, and feeling tired. People with compromised immune systems may experience more serious symptoms and develop pneumonia. Most patients recover in four to six weeks. Rest may be needed for a month or longer.

In newborns, 10 out of every 1,000 babies will have CMV. Nine will have no symptoms, but one may have a more serious illness leading to nervous system damage, developmental disabilities, vision impairment, deafness, or gastrointestinal disease.

The incubation period is 3 to 12 weeks. CMV remains in the body through your whole lifetime. The laboratory test uses a culture to identify the presence of the virus cells and is expensive. There is no vaccine, nor a treatment for the virus.

In patients who have a depressed immune system, CMV-related diseases may be more aggressive. Infection with CMV is a major cause of disease and death in immunocompromised patients, including people with organ transplants and cancer as well as those on dialysis and people who are HIV-infected. Organ transplant patients should minimize their exposure to CMV sources. Transplant teams try to give CMV-negative patients organs and blood products that are free of the virus. Patients without the CMV virus who receive organs from CMV-infected donors are given valganciclovir or ganciclovir and are monitored to see whether the CMV titers increase.

"I will never forget that snowy, December night," Deb Strout told me, "that we got the call that you needed a heart transplant and you would need blood." Deb was one of the people at Betty's party. This is her story . . .

"Rich and I were at the Paldaufs for their annual Holiday Open House. There were a lot of people from the church there, and the Paldaufs got the call that anyone that would like to donate blood to you would need to drive to Children's Hospital immediately. So Rich and I decided that we would just stop by home and then drive to Children's. During that short time, we also discussed asking our son Chris if he would like to come to Children's with us and donate blood. Only one problem: we couldn't find him. He wasn't home like he was supposed to be."

Now you are probably wondering, where was Chris!? This is his story . . .

"I wasn't supposed to be out there.

"The athletic fields were pitch dark, and the lights from the houses on the other side stood in stark relief to the blackness beyond. I can't remember if there were stars, and there was no moon, and the glow I remember most was the burning ember of my cigarette. My parents were off on yet another selfless mission call; I wasn't really sure if it was volunteer ambulance duty or church or something else. It didn't matter: All it meant was I could sneak out of the house and go smoke.

"I was old enough to drive—heck, I was almost 17—but I knew taking the car would be too risky. If I walked, I could sneak a smoke or two as I crossed the fields to the other side, cloaking my illegal activity in

darkness, and then make my way up the back street before looping back for home. I figured a McDonald's shake would be a perfect cover if I got caught.

"*Which, of course, is exactly what happened. Not only did I get caught, I walked into a storm of activity. Every light in the house was on. I knew I was in for it before I even stepped in the door. My brother had covered for me, and, when I came in holding the plastic cup from McDonalds, my alibi was thankfully confirmed. But, although I was able to hide the real reason I had snuck out, the fact is I wasn't home when I was needed.*

"*And my parents needed me. Or, rather, a family we knew needed me. They needed my blood. My dad made me a deal: If I went with him, right now, down to the city, to Children's Hospital, I wouldn't be grounded. Somehow, somewhere along the way, we knew that I had A+ blood, and because I was born in California there was a chance I had "clean" blood— blood that had not been altered by a virus common in colder climates like Chicago. Which, as crazy as it sounded to me at the time, meant that my blood was suitable for transfusion to a newborn.*

I didn't know all the details, but I knew I could help. Being grounded was the least of my worries; here I had the chance to help save someone's life. This family from church had a little girl, and she was very sick, and my blood could make a difference. They had already taken her from our local hospital all the way into the city. It wasn't certain she would live, even with my blood, but there was a chance. And I had to take it."

Resuming with Deb's story:

"The three of us then headed for the hospital. It was snowy and cold, but not too many cars were on the road. Once we got to the hospital, it was around midnight when we found where we were supposed to go and checked in. The lab tech explained to us that they were looking for blood that did not have a certain enzyme. After answering many questions, Rich, Chris, and I donated enough blood so that they could test. They then sent us home and told us that they would give us a call if any of us could donate blood for Lauren's transplant.

"The next day, the call came in that only Chris's blood could be used—so off we went again to the hospital. That was the day you were actually having surgery. Rich and I went to the waiting room, where some of the people from church were waiting for you to have surgery. Chris was in the lab giving blood. After he gave his blood, he then came to the waiting room.

"That was quite an experience; you had many, many, many people on pins and needles and praying for a successful surgery."

Chris:

"The rest of the evening comes and goes in snapshots. I remember sitting in the back of my dad's car, praying harder than I'd ever prayed before, telling God that I would quit smoking if he saved this little girl's life. I remember sitting in the Children's Hospital cafeteria, scared out of my mind that they would find the nicotine in my bloodstream and reject me and tell my dad. I remember being even more scared that I would be accepted, but that the nicotine would somehow cause damage that couldn't be repaired. I remember being excited that my blood didn't have the virus tracing. And I remember sitting in a chair, watching reruns of "The Dukes of Hazard" as my blood slowly filled the bag attached through a tube to my arm."

No wonder I like country! I got a heart from Texas, and I got my blood from a country TV fan!

In my crib at the hospital: "So big!"

Chris continues:

"Lauren survived that night, and the next and the next—when I first saw her, it was her parents' first time back at church, one Sunday morning several weeks or months later. Then I went off to college, and I didn't see her for a long time, until another Sunday morning when she was being precocious and her mom looked like she had her hands full. Then I moved away, and I don't remember whether I've seen her grown up. In my mind, she's that baby, that child, that little girl I helped save.

"I have a little girl of my own now, and someday I'm going to tell her this story. I'm going to take her to McDonald's, just me and her, and I'm going to order us a couple of shakes. I'm going to tell her that, although every baby is born perfect, sometimes babies need a little help. And one time, when her Nana and Grandpa needed me, they couldn't find me right away. But then they did, and we drove a long way to a hospital, and we helped a little baby who was sick to get better. And how that is one of the proudest moments of my life.

"I still have a clipping from the local newspaper, the story and a photo of Lauren swaddled tightly in her mother's arms with her dad looking on. I come across it from time to time as I'm shuffling boxes, and all the old memories come flooding back. I remember that dark night, not being where I was supposed to be, and ultimately being exactly where I needed to be, to help give life to someone in need."

7.

The Mystery of
Barney and Friends

"ABC" by the Jackson 5

Another of my Mom's stories goes like this:

"Standing inches from the eye-level, 15-inch TV, as the Barney melody
started, so did my two-and-a-half-year-old's humming. At the first
break, she dragged the black, two-stair step stool directly in front of
the TV screen, to get ready for her favorite show. 'I love you, you love
me, and we're a happy family' . . . that tune, which annoyed most
adults, was the start of fantasy time with Lauren's friends, Barney and
Baby Bop. Much to my frustration, although I moved the stool a
safe distance from the harmful TV rays that might damage her eyes,
before I got to the next room I would hear the stool being dragged
back to the original location. Her 'hmmmm' was accurate in regards
to the timing, and to the pitch, and as soon as the jingle came on the
television Lauren stopped what she was doing and ran right over to the
screen. During the breaks in the television show, she jabbered in a loud
voice to 'explain' to everyone what Barney's activity of the day had
been. Being large puppets, she was attentive to the characters moving
their mouths, but, other than 'Barney,' Lauren uttered only a few
intelligible words."

Mom was puzzled.

• • • •

Speaking of Barney, I actually had an opportunity to meet him. I was very young. It wasn't even an event for "sick children." I waited for Barney in my own room, with my family. I was happily sitting in a high chair, eating pancakes, directly across from the door through which, soon, Barney would enter. Sue Vetter, who had been a student in Dad's high school math class, arranged this command performance. Filled with anticipation, I was shocked when the door opened and a big *violet*, not purple, dinosaur entered the room. However, it was much larger than me. When the big pastel dinosaur entered my room, I was not happy to see this imposter!

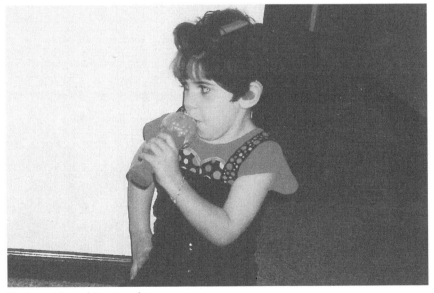

Singing with my big microphone.

I screamed, "You're not Barney! You're the wrong color purple!" Then I threw my pancakes on Barney's tummy. I stubbornly argued with my mom that this was an imposter and a cruel trick to play on a kid, expressed by kicking my legs, crying, and screaming. No one was more surprised than Sue (the lady who arranged the date) that the costume was not as expected, and, although now I appreciate her efforts, I was stumped by the experience.

Isolation

As Mom said, "Due to the need to isolate Lauren from germs, the daily television shows were her link to the outside world. Television provided most of her opportunity for social interaction. These were the only friendships that were safe, ones that didn't jeopardize her fragile health. Being immunosuppressed but also being a growing, learning child who needed experiences to build language skills didn't go hand in hand. We avoided situations that could cause her to become ill—no Sunday school, no preschool, no McDonald's Playland, and no visit with cousins for weeks after they had shots. I wondered why she wasn't more verbal. Most of her speech was unintelligible. She communicated through expressions that caused others to break out in laughter, and allowed us to understand when she became frustrated or sad, or was in pain."

Medication Schedule

Mom continued, "Our daily schedule was filled with medical responsibilities. Anti-rejection drugs, which were given every eight hours, were to be taken on an empty stomach, and eating/drinking was avoided for one hour afterwards. That means, for six hours of the day, food and drink were off limits. This was not easy with a toddler, especially one that was a very picky eater. The drug, cyclosporine, was in a liquid form, and had to be mixed in a glass container with orange juice. A shot glass was the perfect size to mix the drug, which was the consistency of olive oil. In order to get the entire dose, the cyclosporine was mixed with orange juice, drawn into a one-milliliter syringe and expelled into Lauren's mouth. Then a "rinse" of orange juice was poured into the shot glass, swished to mix any residual medication left on the glass, drawn into the syringe and deposited into Lauren's mouth. This was repeated at 8 a.m., 4 p.m., and midnight; it meant orange juice, a syringe, cyclosporine, and a shot glass always had to be available. Varying collections of medications were given at 9 a.m. and 9 p.m. I tell you about this to explain that my whole attention was not on her development. I had to maintain a medical routine, which also included frequent blood draws, to ensure the 'levels' were appropriate. My attention was not fully available to discover why she wasn't communicating.

"Julie, our devoted speech pathologist, brought props, played new games, and used activities to encourage verbalization as well as sign language. We continued informal checks of hearing. We made an appointment to see the educational audiologist. The results of the test were inconclusive.

"If you want to get a quicker diagnosis, your physician can order an ABR—that means auditory brainstem response test. Electrodes would be placed on Lauren's head, and the action of her brain waves would identify her hearing acuity. We would know immediately whether she had a hearing loss.

"Julie worked with other preschool hearing-impaired children. She said, 'Some of the children I work with improved tremendously after they got hearing aids.' I was puzzled because sometimes Lauren seemed to hear, but other times she seemed to be missing things. The possibility of a hearing loss pushed us to schedule an ABR because the possibility of an undiagnosed hearing loss could be delaying communication skills.

"On the test day, a nurse squirted three syringes of pink medicine into Lauren's mouth to make her sleepy. She was restless, but stayed awake. An additional dose did the trick, and she was taken for the evaluation.

A short time later, an audiologist came in to tell me that Lauren was profoundly deaf. Patrick stated as gently as possible, 'She has a profound bi-lateral sensory-neural loss.'

I thought, it is past severe; it's in the profound range: the label of the most severe degree of hearing loss. Both ears are affected, and it couldn't be fixed because the nerves are dead. At this point, Lauren was returned to the small room to wait for the anesthetic to wear off. While the audiologist tried to answer my questions, Lauren began to flail and roll. It was difficult to prevent her from falling off the bed, or striking the wall. This was a very unusual response and very distracting while trying to digest this new diagnosis.

"'Why don't you make a follow-up appointment so we can discuss amplification,' suggested Patrick. I couldn't help but remind Patrick that she could sing on pitch. I wasn't trying to argue the diagnosis, but I couldn't reconcile that fact with the diagnosis. Patrick probably thought I was bargaining—trying to deny the diagnosis. Having been through several traumatic situations with Lauren,

I think acceptance came easier. Perhaps I would have been more shocked and disappointed if the result showed normal hearing. Then I wouldn't have been able to explain the delay in her speech. Patrick tried to give encouragement: 'All children respond differently, and children with this type of hearing loss can do quite well. There are excellent accommodations available. We'll set up an appointment for amplification assessment.' Patrick left, and Lauren continued to throw her body against the wall. The next few hours were exhausting as I tried to restrain Lauren to prevent her from hurting herself.

"I called Julie, Lauren's speech teacher, and told her the news. Julie replied, 'Really. She fooled us! It's a good thing you have been using sign language. We'll step up signing in therapy. You should meet Abbi—she and Lauren would get along, and now they have even more in common.' I hung up, and then I cried."

Hearing Aids for Lauren

For a change, we weren't in the cardiology waiting room. Some mornings, volunteers came by with book carts and I could select any book I wanted! Some days, volunteers had games at a little table where I could play "Don't Break the Ice" or "Connect Four." Some days there were pictures to color while I waited. The television was not usually on when we got there, because it was *so* early. We had to be at the hospital at 7 a.m. This meant, to beat the rush traffic, we left home at 5:45 a.m. That was after staying up to take medicine at midnight! Our little transplant group was scheduled early to miss the crowds that would come later, which would increase the chances that our weakened immune systems might be exposed to something catchy.

Mom said, "Patrick demonstrated the advantages and disadvantages of several types of aids and recommended a behind-the-ear model, given the degree of loss and your age. Patrick told us calmly, 'You will need to keep the spare batteries and the used one in a safe place. They are little and attractive to children. If swallowed, the results can be deadly.'"

Patrick taught Mom how to unlock the compartment that held the #13 zinc battery that I still use today. A couple of weeks later, following a cardiology appointment, we visited Patrick's office and got the hearing aid molds with the new aids.

As Mom told me, Patrick said, "I've programmed the volume to a low setting so that it won't shock Lauren. Unlike glasses that you put on and your vision is corrected, hearing aid use begins with a small increase in volume that the child should be able to tolerate, and then is increased over a period of time." Patrick twisted the new mold into my ear, and asked me to shake my head. The aid didn't fall out.

Then Patrick attempted my first hearing test with aids. Mom remembered, "Knowing that she likes to please, I was not sure whether Lauren was tossing the blocks into the bucket because she knew she was supposed to, or whether her action truly indicated she perceived sound. Patrick suggested I look into hearing aid loss insurance because young children are prone to losing aids. Everybody was smiling and happy, and Patrick gave Lauren some stickers before we headed home.

"When we went outside, you had a puzzled look on your face. You covered her ears as if something was bothering you. You apparently hadn't heard wind before. The same puzzled expression returned when the car started moving. Later, I learned the look was probably due to the fact the hearing aid amplification is not selective. The tires rubbing on the road provided a constant 'whoo, whooo, whoo' that drowned out our voices and music. On this first ride home, I also learned the annoyance of feedback. Driving on the Kennedy during rush hour, with you in your car seat fast asleep, your new hearing aids were screeching in response to the position of the aids in relation to the car seat. It was quite apparent that it would take all of us some time to become accustomed to hearing aid usage."

Education

Mom continued, "The diagnosis of profound hearing loss brought a new challenge. Your hearing loss qualified you for a language classroom through the low-incidence special education public school program beginning at age 3. This was in conflict with the plan for children who have had infant heart transplants. The transplant team told us their goal was to see you go to kindergarten. 'We believe,' argued Dr. Zales, 'children will come out of surgery will the ability with which they went into surgery. That being said, we don't know much about the strengths and weaknesses of each because they are so young. We don't believe there will be long-term adverse effects from the transplant or the medication. We look forward to seeing Lauren thrive, and go to kindergarten! With better understanding of follow-up care, improvements in drugs, infections and rejection—both acute and chronic—could be warded off for longer survival.' Because the rule was to avoid children who had shots, and to avoid chicken pox, starting school at age three was not what the cardiologists had in mind.

"No parents are happy about sending three-year-olds on a bus trip one hour each way, to an all-day school program. I wasn't willing to trust the system to get you the correct medication consistently on time. How could I arrange your medication so the dosing wouldn't fall during school hours? Added to the time spent in medical follow up, I felt too much of your day would be spent on a bus.

"After searching, I became aware of another preschool for deaf children just north of our home in Crystal Lake." After arguing her case, just the beginning of becoming my strongest advocate, the school system allowed me to attend the closer school even though it was out of district.

"The first time I drove you to visit the preschool class," Mom continued, "you sat in your car seat, sucking your fingers, and seemed to be contemplating the idea of school. You had been isolated, and I wasn't sure of how you would react, being suddenly plunged into a classroom full of children. When we arrived at South School, the room was a flurry of activity. There were several inviting centers, a cash register, and a dress-up area. Your eyes opened very wide, as if you were seeing a magical, secret place like the North Pole toy workshop with elves busy at work. Still reserved, you pointed, as if to ask, 'Do I go in there?' I nodded, and you took off to join in.

"In order to get you to leave, I said, 'You need a backpack and a lunch box so you can be part of the class. We need to go get them.' In fact, there were many details that needed to be ironed out before you could attend.

"As with the first day of school for any child, the mothers are proud, happy, and apprehensive. In addition to the usual emotions, hanging over my head was the problem of additional germ exposure. If you were exposed to chicken pox, you needed *painful* shots within 24 hours to decrease the severity of an outbreak. The shots might save your life. In the future there was a possibility that there would be a vaccination to eliminate chicken pox. The problem was, Lauren, you would be attending a school full of kids who could have chicken pox, and exposure leading to organ rejection was a very real possibility.

"You would be the first transplanted infant to attend public preschool. This was not because you were the oldest; it was because you needed to start earlier due to your hearing loss. The team figured their little transplant baby patients would have five years before they had to develop a plan to deal with the germs from school populations. The heart transplant co-coordinator, Sherri, took time to drive out to your new school to meet with the teacher and nurse. This caring, dedicated staff devoted hours to making the plan work. If I had to pay them hourly, I couldn't have afforded all the time people put into making this a safe and successful experience. This included informing all the parents that, if their child got chicken pox, they needed to call our family *immediately*, because a life-saving shot had to be administered within the first 24 hours after exposure if it would have a chance to prevent organ rejection. There was a CPR refresher for teachers, and meetings with the school nurse. There was a lot of paperwork for the hospital and teachers, a lot of planning—but, once completed, you went to school.

"You *loved* Bedell. 'B hand sign' was dedicated to helping families adjust to educating their hearing-impaired children, and helping families to learn sign right along with them. The school's activities immersed you in opportunities to increase your language skills. Bedell organized summer camp, picnics, parties, and holiday celebrations where we could improve our ASL. This built a close friendship among the families."

The Trials of Hearing Aids

As Mom noted, "Your first pair of hearing aids was analogue. They amplified all the high and low frequencies equally. The only adjustment was how the volume was set, or a switch that controlled on and off. You have an unusual loss; at the low frequencies your hearing was nearly normal. As the frequencies got higher, your perception is worse until, at the highest speech-range frequencies, you couldn't hear sounds at the loudest volume the machine could produce. Although you hear low sounds, you know it is hard for you to hear speech. You couldn't hear birds chirping; you can't hear someone if they whisper. Sounds like 's,' 'z,' 'sh,' 'f,' or 'th' are mysteries.

"Technology was not advanced enough to compensate for a loss such as yours. The problem was, any increase to improve your high frequencies loss resulted in over-amplification in the low frequencies, which probably resulted in pain. Do you recall all the times we had to search for hearing aids?"

I remember some places I "lost" them:

- threw the aids somewhere in the grass in Alex's yard.
- took them off at the playground and left them under the slide.
- tossed the pain makers in the garbage without anyone noticing, at the mall.
- hid one pair in the bottom of a flashlight, and threw out the batteries.
- tossed the aids into the lake, and watched the pretty circles they made in the water before they sunk to the bottom, never to be found.

"Trying to coax you into liking the aids," Mom continued, "Patrick let you choose bright hot pink ear molds for the next pair. By this time, technology was making some advances, giving us hope that the newer aids would be more useful.

"A new digital model came out that could amplify the high and low sounds separately. Everyone thought we had solved the problem. $5,000 later, with hot pink molds and new digital hearing aids, everyone looked at you expectantly. We wished your response would be, 'I can hear. I love them. I will learn to speak clearly and catch up on all the language I have missed. Thank you for finding the perfect solution. Thank you for not giving up on hearing aids when I threw all the old ones away.' In reality, these hearing aids did not work much better, and thanks to a law that said you could return hearing aids after a trial period, the hearing aids were returned."

One advantage of my sloping, precipitous hearing loss is that my voice quality was nearly normal. Some people think I have an accent: 'Are you from New York?' Some people think I have a cold. Most of the time, people understand me. But at times, I become frustrated when people 'forget' that I can't hear.

"When you were first diagnosed," Mom said, "I wanted to say you are hard of hearing, as if that wasn't as much of a problem as compared to being labeled deaf. Now, I'd like you to wear a baseball cap that says 'deaf' on the back to remind people to speak to your face to allow you to lip-read."

People who don't have a hearing loss think when they see a person wearing something in their ear that they are fixed. In fact, we are struggling to make sense out of whatever is bombarding our ears. Hearing aids amplify all sounds equally. The buzz of a fan, the tires in the car, or the buzz in lights is amplified equally to voices in the room. In a lunchroom, the trays clanking behind hearing aid wearers are as loud as the person sitting in front of them talking. The people tapping their feet, or rocking their chairs and making clicks when the legs hit the floor, the broom-brushing sounds, and the fan noise all add together for chaos.

"Just as Patrick predicted," Mom continued, "when you were three years old, you, like many other hearing-impaired children, were doing well with accommodations. And there will be technological advances, and perhaps even nerve implants or genetic engineering, in the future. Maybe someday, you will hear the birds' chirp, just as your favorite Disney character, Snow White, did."

This thought is typical of a hearing parent of a deaf child. While children are very young, parents are faced with many decisions. They must try to predict which option will be optimal for their child: ASL, ASL/speech, or speech. Do hearing children of deaf parents face similar questions? Deaf advocates warn that hearing parents' decisions may be based on audism (a term to describe types of discrimination against deafness and deaf people.) Deaf people may be offended by a parent's choice to use cochlear implants because their viewpoint firmly maintains that deafness is *not* an illness to be cured. Deafness is viewed as a culture, not a disease that needs a medical fix. Parents soon recognize that communication could divide their family now, or later. My parents chose to try both channels and see what my reaction would be.

8.
The "No-No" List
"Breakaway" by Kelly Clarkson

Better safe than sorry; here is a list of things transplant patients must avoid. Some could lead to rejection, while others could make any person with a transplant sick.

Things that could lead to rejection
1. Turtles—they can carry Salmonella bacteria
2. Bird mites
3. Mold
4. Blue cheese
5. Aspergillus (molds)
6. The body's response to a foreign material—even a splinter!
7. Chicken pox
8. Too much leukocyte action (white blood cells)—the transplant medicine works on lowering white blood cell count
9. Cryptosporidium (a parasite that can contaminate water)
10. Viruses
11. Being around kids who recently received live vaccinations such as MMR
12. Scuba diving
13. Being in a hot tub

14. Construction and renovation projects—especially when they're ripping out old materials.
15. Live vaccines.
16. Sick people

My parents, being parents, stayed on top of this stuff, teaching it to the rest of the family and eventually to me. Just as all parents want their children to be happy and independent, mine were no different. This doesn't mean they haven't cringed as I've begun to go out on my own and take charge of my daily medications, keeping my own watchful eye, and hopefully making smart choices.

Unfortunately, this list was not available when I had my transplant. In 1989, transplantation was still a new medical option for infants. It was trial and error, and I was the youngest baby to have had a transplant. The team—that is, the doctors and my parents—spent a lot of time sorting out what was "normal" baby response and what was transplant related.

Many transplant babies like me would learn the hard way about things that could make them sick or lead to a heart rejection.

One other important observation: the use of ibuprofen is discouraged, because it is hard on the kidneys, which are forced to take a beating from the anti-rejection drugs.

9.
Chips and Cheese
"Upside Down" by Jack Johnson

"Are we going to Chips and Cheese house?" I asked Mom.

I loved getting in the car to go to Chips and Cheese house. Sitting in the back seat of Dad's "old mobile" (really an Oldsmobile), I wiggled my rear on the very comfortable seat, one that could easily lull me to sleep even on short rides. Our favorite mechanic knew how much my Dad loved what he called the "couch-mobile," not only for the comfy interior but also because it got 28 miles to the gallon. Dad loved it so much that when his first Delta Eighty-Eight topped 200,000 miles, although it ran like a champ, he began contemplating a replacement. This consideration was forced because the manufacturer had dropped the beloved Eighty-Eight model. One day we were driving past Santa's Village (a mini-version of a giant amusement park) and, while I was focused on the giant candy cane and Santa statue at the entrance, Dad's attention was drawn to a sparkling gray replica of his beige beauty on a GM lot right next door. We drove right in and bought it. Though Dave and I referred to the Delta Eighty-Eight as "the boat," I have to admit we could fit a lot of stuff in the enormous trunk when packing for vacations. Plus, the ample room in the back seat provided enough room for both my brother and me to spread out and sleep comfortably on our summer adventures. On the other hand, I never went to sleep when we were headed to see Chips and Cheese— i.e., my grandparents.

I was so excited! First, we went over a bridge that has a dam underneath it. I always got nervous when the car was on the bridge because I was afraid I would fall into the churning river. I was relieved and happy once the car was off the bridge and on the curvy road that winds into a hilly pine tree forest and leads to Grandpa and Grandma's house. I didn't know how to say Grandma or Grandpa yet, but because they always had my favorite snack—Sun Chips and spray cheese—I called them Chips and Cheese, as that was much easier for me to remember how to say.

At Chips and Cheese house, I always ate my Sun Chips and spray cheese on a yellow heart-shaped plate. I drank my water or grape juice from my Snow White cup. Grandma always had little cups of healthy snacks like carrots cut into quarters or crinkle sticks waiting to tempt me. Dave ate off of a white plate like our parents, but Chips and Cheese got me a special plate to remind me that I am special. When I wanted a drink, I grabbed the clear plastic cup that had Snow White's face on it and asked Chips or Cheese to pour some drink in the cup.

I also ate at a different table than everyone else. They sat at the big table with a green tablecloth, fancy forks, spoons, and knives. They let me eat at a table that was my height and closer to the TV so I could look at the faces because no one had closed-captioning.

I didn't know the term yet, but I was hard-of-hearing. When I stood next to the big table, I had to look up to see the top. If I stood next to my table, I could look down to see my special plate and cup. My table was red and square, but the big table was round like the mirror in my bedroom.

When I was done eating, I usually went downstairs to play in my special place. I ran eagerly, my feet squashing the shag carpeting that was green as grass. Everything in the house was green except my special place, which was a vanity that Cheese had given me. There was a three-way mirror with beveled glass that my mom had in her room when she was growing up. My special place included the super-sized Barbie doll standing by the dresser. My grandma had another doll, Patti Playpal, which belonged to my mother. If you held her hands a special way, she walked with you. I had to be gentle, because Patti's head had a way of snapping back, and no one wanted Patti to break. On the dresser was a big Barbie head. I combed her yellow hair and put Cheese's make-

Grandpa and Grandma Sumner—i.e., Chips and Cheese.

up on Barbie's face, including lipstick and pink round circles on her cheeks. I enjoyed having some quiet time to myself.

"Laur, want to go fishing with Dave and me?" Dad yelled. Chips and Cheese's house was right on a lake.

"Fishy!" I said, dropping the lipstick and running out the sliding glass doors, still wearing my princess crown after dressing up like a "Pretty, Pretty Princess." The name came from this game that you won by accumulating and wearing all the pieces in a set of princess jewelry. Maybe the shiny metal would attract fish like Dad's lures that I couldn't touch. We walked back to the pier so that Dave, Dad, and I could get into the drab green fishing boat. I preferred the color of the bright yellow Sunfish sailboat that sat on the shore.

"Laur, put your arms out," Dad said. "I need to put the life jacket on you."

Instead, I crossed my arms in front of my chest, stood firm, and shook my head, refusing to help my dad put on that orange jacket. It was not comfy. I felt like a bloated clown fish, like Nemo, when I wore it. "No, thank you!"

"If you don't put it on, then you're not going on the boat trip with us," he stated sternly.

I succumbed and put my arms out, and, after the jacket was on, I grabbed my pink princess fishing pole. I was determined to catch a fish. Bluegills were my favorite to catch because they were so cute!

Chips and Cheese lived on a lake that was very good for catching pan fish. The cove behind their house was a prime spawning spot; in the spring, you got a hit as soon as your pole was in the water. Near the shore, you could see the saucers the pan fish excavate. The colony of craters was filled with dancing males early in the season and gazillions of minnows soon after. All this action held the attention of little kids like me, because you could see the swirls on top of the water. The drawback was that a few feet out from the prime spawning area was dense algae.

"Oh, I got a fishy!" Dad grabbed the pole and line and pulled it in for me. I was so excited that I caught one first! Dad reeled up my catch because I was in frenzy from my quick success.

"It's coming. Hold on, Laur!" Dad's face was making a bunch of wrinkles as he scrunched in concentration and a little aggravation. My dad is famous for shortening names. He is a fast-paced man; he walks fast and talks fast, so long names are a nuisance to him. Caryn is Care, Alison is Al, Thomas is T, but he can't shorten Dave.

I jumped up and down in the rowboat, unable to contain my excitement. I shrieked and clapped my hands.

"Lauren, you are rocking the boat," my brother warned. "Settle down, or you will scare the fish away!"

Then I saw green stems and leaves of seaweed. "Where fishy?"

"There was a fish in the seaweed, because I saw the fin," said Dad, trying to mellow my disappointment. "He escaped to grow bigger!"

I was so sad that I started crying.

My brother suddenly shouted, "Lauren, I got one! Come help me!" I dropped my pink fishing pole and scrambled over the middle seat to help my brother pull the fish from the water. My tears were fading as I saw big splashes in the water. And then, very quickly, because we were fishing in a shallow area, a fish appeared.

"Yay! It's a bluegill!" I said loudly. Everything I said was quite loud, not because of my enthusiasm but because of my hearing loss. My voice was high pitched, piercing, and loud most of the time. Some might have confused this with persistent enthusiasm, but loud speech is a trait of my hearing loss.

My brother rolled his eyes and gave me the minnow-sized fish, anxious to catch a bigger one. On the other hand, my elation was apparent as I grabbed the fish and squealed, "I name it Froggy!" I petted the slimy, flopping fish, admiring and examining my prize. I easily slid my finger right in Froggy's mouth as Dad taught me and shouted "cheese!" as if I was having my picture taken. Then I kissed Froggy right on the lips. Daddy didn't like me doing that. He was worried about my immune system and stuff making me sick.

Before the sun went down (probably only 30 minutes later, but it seemed like half a day), we headed back to Chips and Cheese's house. We put the boat belonging to Uncle Marge and Aunt Stan (as I mistakenly called them) back on shore. We had an anchor in case it flooded, but I thought it was rather silly to have an anchor attached to the boat on the shore. Dad told Davey to stand with me on the dock as he packed all his fishing gear.

"Orange off now!" I shouted. But daddy wouldn't let me take off the blow-up orange jacket until we got off the short, gray dock.

"No, not until we get off the dock. Okay?" my brother instructed patiently. "Dad's almost done packing the fishing supplies. We can help bring things up to the garage. Did you have fun fishing today?"

Before I even got to answer, my father answered for me. Like I said, he rushes things in life.

"Wow, your fish was very cool-looking!" said Dad, sweat running down his forehead from the hot summer day. He was wearing his White Sox baseball hat to protect his eyes from the sun. Dave wore the same kind of hat, but I still proudly wore my pretty, pretty princess crown. My light-up Velcro gym shoes flashed red lights as I walked under the giant willow trees that provided shade from the bright sunlight.

At last, Dad took off my life jacket, and I ran as fast as I could to the tree house. Strips of wood were nailed onto the tree trunk as a ladder. I would start climbing, get to the third rung, and then I couldn't go up anymore. I always had to wait for help because the next rung was spaced too far for my legs. The tree house belonged to my friend, also named Lauren, who lived two houses down from where Chips and Cheese live. I didn't see her often, but her younger brother went to school with Dave. I thought it was cool we had the exact same name. She reminded me of Pippi Longstocking when I first met her, because she had red hair, often in braids, and tons of freckles. She played soccer, just like me, although she was better than I was because she's older. Sometimes, she went outside to blow bubbles and talk to me. The first time I met her, she told me I could go to her tree house whenever I wanted.

"Lauren, time for medicine! Come inside," my mom yelled from far away.

I rolled my eyes dramatically and pouted all the way back to the house, until I saw Chips waving to me from the upper balcony. As soon as I saw him, I raced toward the house, rushing to beat Davey. Dave was really fast, but then he stopped and gave me a friendly tickle. As my brother hugged me from behind, I wrestled free, grinning widely and yelling, "Ha ha, surprise!" His tickling and my giggling were unstoppable until I was exhausted.

I took my medicine, cyclosporine, as a mix. Mom squirted the medicine, which tasted like olive oil, into a shot glass of orange juice. I drank the mix along with another shot glass full of orange juice to make sure I got all the medicine.

The drug, which prevents organ rejection, actually comes from a fungus found in the soil of Norway and Switzerland. People who had transplants before cyclosporine was discovered died. This was true until just a few years before my birth. Used successfully on adults, the next frontier was children. Cyclosporine was approved for treatment in 1983, and pioneered on a 28-year-old woman in Pittsburgh. I have taken medicine all my life. I carry cute purple lunch bags with baby bottles of orange juice, oral syringes, and shot glasses; the medicine has to be mixed in glass because it sticks to plastic. I take this orange juice and oil mixture four times a day, never missing a dose by more the 30 minutes. I get my first dose at eight in the morning, then four in the afternoon, and when I was young my mom stayed up until midnight every night to give me the last dose.

In addition, I got a few pills in the morning with Poly-Vi-Flor, the worst tasting stuff ever. However, I do like the liquid Bactrim that helps prevent thrush in my mouth. At night, I get a couple more pills. The last thing my dad says every time we leave the house is, "Medicine?"

After outdoor fun, I ran through the green family room, up the green stairs, and took a right to get to the green living room. I ran to sit on Chip's lap. He was sitting in the biggest chair in the house; it was made of dark green leather. He asked, "You want an apple cheek, Lauren?"

"Yes!"

When we were finished eating apples, it was story time. My mom tells me how much I loved hearing my grandfather's stories. He could settle me down with his descriptive and interactive storytelling.

"Once upon a time, a girl named . . . What was her name, Lauren?" (I usually chose my own name so I could be part of the adventure.) He continued, "A girl named Lauren walked down a path. On both sides of the path, she could see tall trees made of candy. The candy trees were very sweet. They were . . . What color were they, Lauren?"

"Purple!" I shouted.

"The purple candy trees shaded the path to the candy house. It was covered with all kinds of treats, like carrots!"

"Not carrots, Chips, candy!"

Soon, I rested my head against Chips, started sucking my fingers and rubbing my ear, and, before the princess got to the candy house, I fell asleep. I relaxed and drifted off feeling secure, loved, and very happy.

10.
Christmas Eve 1995
"Wonderful Christmastime" by Paul McCartney

I was six years old.

I was inspired to read more books after enjoying story time with Mom, Dad, Chips, and sometimes even Dave. The Christmas of 1995, there was one thing on my Christmas list.

When it was time to open presents with Chips, Cheese, Uncle Marge, Aunt Stan (Why couldn't I get this right?), Christine, Ann Louise, and my family, I was in charge of handing out the gifts. I was Santa's little helper. I even wore an apron that said *Santa's Little Helper*. I wore a hat with pointed ears that looked like elves' ears. Dave dressed as Santa. We are the babies of the family. After giving presents to other members of the family, I opened all of the ones with my name. Then, Chips pulled out a present from behind him as if it was magic.

"I have one last present for you," he said.

The present was hard and wrapped with princess wrapping paper. I was excited and couldn't even remember what I had requested. But Chips knew what I wanted for Christmas—he gave me the book *Alice in Wonderland*. It was no surprise that the storyteller himself gave me a book for Christmas.

Cheese (Grandma) had a contagious smile, spoke several languages, could solve all the crossword puzzles, was kind, and always tried to help those in need. My dad feels this quote fits the description of my grandma: "She's the closest human being I know to God."

She was honest, loveable, and a fantastic poker player. All the men said she could really bluff! She made all the grandchildren a fabulous gingerbread house every year. But at the age of 94 she passed away, the week of my junior prom.

She made the detailed decorations from scratch. The sides of the house had heart-shaped windows made from candy canes. The roof was covered with gummy candy and Santa's sleigh and reindeer. My favorite part was the snowman outside the house that came from my favorite candy store, Fannie Mae. There were fake silver balls around the windows and house to look like Christmas lights. The sidewalk that led to the front door was made of M&M candies.

Chips told the story of candy land, while Cheese made candy land come to life in her own special way.

Sadly, I don't personally remember any of the stories I just told you. A mistake happened. My parents' worst nightmare became reality.

One of my Grandma's spectacular gingerbread houses.

11.
Lost in Wonderland
Alice in Wonderland Soundtrack by Vitaliy Zavadskyy

Memory . . . is the diary that we all carry about with us.
—Oscar Wilde

As I said, I was six years old. Sitting straight in my chair, my head was held high. The loud, annoying bell rang through the speakers in the classroom. The ceilings were low for adults, but not from the perspective of a first-grader. Short, royal blue lockers lined the hallways. The usual congestion slowed all who were eager to escape for a few moments of rest and relaxation. Kids ran out the doors. Noises came from every direction. Running in the dark hallway, the hardwood doors to the outside appeared before me. My pretty pink nails pushed against the gold lever to open the doors. Finally, the sunshine was visible, flooding back into the dark hallway to help my classmates see where they were going. Charging like a bull, my mushroom-style hair bounced toward the blue sky. Running past the already-filled swing sets, I headed straight to the area filled with wood chips next to the soccer field. I was eager to go down my favorite navy blue slide. The shocks that sparked there, in my mind, were reactions due to my abundant head of hair and the hair on my arms.

Suddenly, an image popped into my head, and I slowed down. The light-up Velcro shoes stopped blinking for a moment. Students from first through fifth grade were running around me; everything looked blurry, like a smeared painting. For an instant, motion stopped and sound was absent. But there was one student who was perfectly clear. She had yellow hair that shined so brightly that it was as if a star was above her head.

I don't remember much about that moment, but I do remember being confused, wanting to go down my favorite slide and, at the same time, trying to remember someone from my past.

Princesses Lauren and Abbi!

I had a flashback to when I was three. I was in a classroom, and I began to move my small feet, running like a bird that has just found her mother. I was flooded with memories. Abbi was handing me plastic fruits that she, my pretend customer, wanted to purchase. How much fun it was to forcefully press the numbers on the red cash register. Next, a vision of us playing dress-up. We were Ariel from *The Little Mermaid* and Jasmine from *Aladdin*. However, the image of her hair returned because it was so incredibly memorable—beautiful and blond with chunks of it sticking out like Pebbles Flinstone. Playing store and dress-up were our favorite pastimes in the preschool class led by Bedell. Not Mrs., not Miss, just Bedell. A 'b' hand sign.

Returning to the playground, my memory was jarred. I focused hard on the blond girl. Was it the girl in my memory? I screamed something like, "Abbi, Abbi! It's you, I know you!" Only the girl didn't look happy, and she stared at me strangely. I had made a mistake. Worse, this was not the return of my memory that I yearned for so intensely.

Then the girl spoke to me, gently and very hesitantly.

"My name is not Abbi. It's Kelsi."

Kelsi recalls saying this to me because she found it strange that I thought I knew her, odd that I thought she was someone else. This is how I must operate now, in a constant state of confusion.

• • • •

But this mistake is not as strange as it seems. It has a history. It was April 1996 when my hometown basketball team, the Chicago Bulls, set a new NBA record for the most wins in a season, achieving their 70th victory. The famous, handsome basketball star, Michael Jordan, was playing for the Bulls at that time. Everyone in Chicago was wearing a white jersey with a red "23" on the front and "Jordan" on the back. Shoes were "Air Jordan's." He was famous for being a great basketball player because it seemed as if he was suspended in air for a long time when he took a shot. His Nike slogan, "Just do it." His movie, *Space Jam*.

I was six years old. My legs were crossed as I sat at the end of my lavender bed. I was watching my favorite show, *The Brady Bunch*. I was fascinated with Cindy Brady, the youngest daughter and my favorite character. My mother often braided my hair in pigtails the way Cindy wore hers. I wanted to be just like her.

And that's the last thing I remember from before it happened.

• • • •

It started early the next morning. After going to bed with a cold and sleeping for a while, I went into my parents' room for a little comfort. I didn't wake them as I climbed in, positioning myself right in the middle. Sleep came quickly. In the morning, my dad tried to wake me. He was shocked to see that one of my pupils was dilated while the other was normal. He shook me, but there was no response. It was very quiet at home that morning. My mom dialed the pediatrician's phone

number. When the answering service picked up, she said, "What
am I doing? I need an ambulance!" While my parents waited for an
ambulance, they were tormented, wondering why they could see my
chest moving up and down but no other signs of life. The ambulance
took me to the closest local hospital. Amazingly, compassionately,
somehow Dr. Kauffman was there waiting for me.

I was transferred to Children's Hospital downtown in very critical
condition. For three days, the doctors examined me and did tests
while using medicines to kill infections. They looked at my brain, but
it didn't show any bleeding, which would have indicated a stroke. My
brain wasn't swollen, at least not yet.

They asked my parents if I could have taken pills, eaten poison,
been around lead-based paint, fallen, or been bitten by a tick. *A tick?*
The labs tests kept showing what wasn't wrong. And I just lay there; no
expression, no movement, a blank.

On the third day, much to the relief of my parents and the medical
team, I woke up. I was terrified. You know how, when you are just
waking up, for a minute you don't remember where you are? On this
day, that minute didn't stop. I had no understanding of what had
happened or what was going on, but, worse than that, there was no
way for me to communicate. My body didn't respond to my desire to
move. *What the heck?*

The night before, wearing a favorite lime green tank top, I
innocently went to bed after watching *The Brady Bunch*. Three
days later, though time was unclear to me, I woke up in a hospital
gown with tubes all over. Some were familiar, like oxygen, but there
were others for food and medicine too. I tried to sit up in bed, but
I couldn't move. I could turn my head, and when my eyes moved
toward my parents, they immediately came over to the bed. The nurses
and doctors came over also. They were all smiling and shaking their
heads. *What was there to be so happy about? I can't move!*

It was so frustrating, I started to cry. When a tear ran down
my cheek, my mom looked upset. Moving my fingers, I spelled the
question, "What happened to me? How long have I been here? Why
can't I move?"

The room where I awoke had four white walls, a chair that folded
out into a bed for my father to nap in, a bed for the prisoner (me),

and a bedside table. It looked like a rehab institution for psychiatric patients. I was terrified of a weird-looking creature staring me in the face—a big stuffed cat was on my bed when I woke up. To this prisoner, a scream seemed appropriate with that thing staring at me, but my voice wouldn't cooperate. The cat had a fake smile sewn on, a round nose, and button eyes. It looked threatening to me. People meant well, sending get-well gifts, but this just added to my fear. *If only I could remember! But remember . . . what?*

Music was coming from somewhere—there, over on the side, from a teddy bear someone had sent. All of this just added to my confusion and feeling of panic. Wanting to escape this imprisonment, I tried moving the rest of my body parts, but I felt only numbness. My arms could move, but nothing below my waist. It was so unreal. Without balance, it was impossible to sit up. *What was going on?*

Intravenous feeding was not very satisfying, but with the possibility of choking, my chart said "NPO." *How is that the abbreviation for "nothing by mouth"?* Not only was everything a puzzle to me, my condition was a puzzle to everyone. My heart was functioning perfectly fine, a big relief to the cardiologists. It was up to the infectious disease and neurology teams to solve the mystery.

After some time—it's hard to say how long, as I was falling in and out of sleep—I was gradually able to swallow thick liquids. Just days before, I had been in the first grade; suddenly I couldn't accomplish the simplest tasks that babies can master.

The next few days were a discovery process. The hospital staff tried to figure out what I could or couldn't do, what medicine would help me, and my prognosis. My parents tried to help me get along in the meantime. Nurses noted, "Patient cannot sit without falling over. Patient cannot move arms or legs." The speech therapist verified that the swallowing reflex was present. Her orders were, "Feeding should be attempted very slowly to prevent food aspiration." No one wanted food getting into my lungs, which could have caused pneumonia. *If only they could do something about this intense headache!*

Frustrated with my inability to communicate, I was even more disturbed that I didn't know much. There was no information to share. If the word had been in my vocabulary, it would have been amnesia. All I could muster was moving my eyes back and forth across the room. Confusion and sadness haunted me. At least both pupils had returned to the same size. When my brother visited, I was happy to see someone more my age. But I couldn't tell him what was going on. I didn't know.

I got a little stronger each day and could soon breathe on my own again, so away went the oxygen. The IV feeding continued, but therapy began to help me swallow thick liquids like gelatin and pudding without choking. I was moved out of intensive care and to a different isolation room. The room was decorated with wooden cutouts of fish, waves, and the sun, and it had striped curtains in pale blue, yellow, orange, and green that covered a window to an adjoining room. There, another child was dealing with a significant challenge, one that required separation from others. My metal hospital bed had bars to prevent me from falling out, but the cage obstructed my view. The television was up high, so at least that view was clear. Every time someone entered the room, focusing through the bars became my challenge. I often missed what was said or happening because it was too difficult to focus, so I just closed my eyes.

I don't remember if I could taste anything, but eating therapy was better than just lying in bed. Two of the therapist's ways of keeping my attention were to give me foods of different temperatures and textures. Eventually, it became interesting to watch TV. The hospital had Disney movies playing, which I liked; however, I couldn't hear and I couldn't read, so the captioning didn't help. It was alright that sleep overpowered me frequently, because I couldn't do much anyway.

My family brought home movies and pictures, which added to my confusion. As people came to visit, I started to learn who they were. Mom would say, "Look who's here! It's Uncle George, the popcorn maker!" *But I couldn't have popcorn yet.*

"Look who's here! It's Aunt Kathy!" Aunt Kathy always wanted to comb my hair because she was a hairdresser, but my hair was so thick that it hurt to get out the tangles. However, I couldn't stop her, so when I saw her, I would start to cry thinking she was going to get the comb out right then. Once the tears started, I couldn't stop, even with reassurance that Aunt Kathy hadn't brought her comb or brush.

My other Aunt Kathy visited and talked to me, but, without any understanding of what she was saying, there was only appreciation for her soothing tone. Aunt Donna always lightened my mood. She would bring paper plates, colorful napkins, and party hats for our pretend picnics.

My grandma had tears in her eyes. My other grandma told me, "We will be playing bingo again soon, and before you know it, we'll be home!" *Oh dear, home? Where is that?* It would be good to get out of the hospital, because they came and woke me up all the time to take my blood pressure, listen to my heart, and get blood samples.

Finally, the doctors told my family I had encephalitis. Dr. Zales, my favorite cardiologist, was very reassuring to my parents: "Her heart is strong and looks good." But Dr. R, a pediatric neurologist, informed us, "Her brain is swollen, and the source of the infection is unclear." Mom later told me that he never looked at me; instead, he looked at his papers the whole time. The infectious disease team continued to try and identify what imbalance in my lab work could explain the source of this condition.

My mommy tried explaining to me that my brain got sick, that my body got something called bacterial meningitis. It turned into encephalitis and, in my case, caused my brain to erase my memory. I was the scarecrow without a brain from the wonderful movie *The Wizard of Oz*. I felt like a girl lost in a scary wonderland. *Where am I? What is going to happen to me? Who am I anyway?*

Ten children in one hundred thousand get meningitis. Fewer kids are supposed to get it now that there are the HiB and MMR vaccinations. In fact, the cause of encephalitis has shifted because the kids who are vaccinated aren't getting measles, mumps, and rubella, so the cases of encephalitis caused by those diseases are disappearing. Adenoviruses and enteroviruses now are the likely causes. Apparently, it's not uncommon for encephalitis and meningitis to occur together, because there is a name for that: meningoencephalitis. That's what I had. Seven percent of the children who get it die. Some go deaf (I was already hard-of-hearing due to the toxic medication I was on while waiting for a new heart at seven days old.). Some kids have seizures later. In kids like me with weak immune systems, this disease grows fast.

After a couple of weeks in the hospital, it was finally time to go home—another strange adventure. I was discharged because the doctors didn't know what else they could do, and they thought I might recover faster in familiar surroundings. If I had been older, I would have been sent to a rehabilitation center. Armed with an IV pole, bags of medicine, a wheelchair, and the scary animals, we headed to Algonquin, Illinois, home to the Pottawatomie Indians and me.

• • • •

Although my bed was soft and there were toys to play with, the IV was my companion every four hours. It was weird to have a place in my arm where Mom put something, but it didn't hurt. I just had to sit and wait until this ball of stuff emptied. A nurse came to help her at first, but then Mom did the IV by herself every four hours. Most of the time, I just sat and looked out the window. Gradually, I began to make out activity in the playground across the street. As the children came and went from school, and while they played at recess, I became

My Aunt Donna!

aware that there was more interesting stuff to look at every day. My understanding grew of what was happening. Though there still wasn't much movement in my limbs, I could eat again and talk a little.

My daily schedule included physical therapy, speech therapy, or sessions with a social worker. I wasn't sure what a social worker was— she was just someone who wanted to talk with me. Sometimes, there would be tears of frustration just trying to talk. Sometimes, the tears were from the irritation brought on by physical therapy. A constant requirement was holding on to the thick wooden bars on either side of me, the kind ballerinas in their pointy, pink shoes use to practice. Hate isn't a strong enough word to describe how much I disliked holding on to those wooden bars trying to force my legs to move, but they wouldn't because they felt numb. It annoyed me to be told how to walk; I liked doing things my own way. However, these things were necessary so that I could learn to do things on my own again.

When another patient walked in for physical therapy, I felt humiliated. Being a kid, it mattered to me what other people thought. When someone walked into the physical therapy center, I would stop pushing my legs to move. The only reason I remember this is because it was an activity that was repeated over and over, enough times for me to memorize it.

Then there was speech with Julie. She showed me a photograph of two girls, me and another girl she said was named Abbi. We were posing like princesses on the soft blue carpet in my living room. I was dressed in my teal and gold princess outfit with my belly button showing, just like Jasmine's from the movie *Aladdin*. I was giving a big, closed-lip smile and showing off my new outfit, complete with a stuffed replica of Raja, the tiger in the movie. On my right side was a girl wearing a violet shirt and laughing. She had blonde hair and brown eyes, and her delightful smile showed off her one missing tooth.

"Lauren, do you remember this girl?" my speech therapist asked.

"Um, no."

Julie asked again, "Don't you remember your friend, Abbi? You took speech together."

Frustrated, again I said, "No!"

Julie then explained that Abbi and I used to share speech therapy sessions. Because I was hard-of-hearing, I often mispronounced words. For example, I had a hard time hearing the "s" sound in words. I remember it was difficult saying "sail." To a hearing person, if I said a word like "sail," it probably sounded like "ail." Speech was a place where I could focus on saying words and sentences clearly. Julie and I signed to each other as we used our voices to communicate. Sometimes, I would use Julie's hands as a reference to catch what she said if I didn't understand what was coming out of her mouth.

This is how confusing everything was, but things would be repeated so they would stick in my memory. Hopefully, they would stick.

Then, my brain started to shrink. At this point, that was a good thing because it was the swelling causing the awful headache. It caused photophobia (sensitivity to light) and messed with my vision, even causing hallucinations. My muscles were wacky too, so I couldn't predict how to move. Dr. R said my central nervous system had been affected. But now, because the cerebrum wasn't so swollen, my headaches got better. Finally, I was behaving more like a six-year-old!

Having seen the pictures of myself playing with Abbi and my cousins so many times, I wanted to see some kids besides those on TV. Mom decided to take me to visit school. *Hmmm.* She said it was the place by the playground that I could see from the window. My brother used to go there.

"You practiced soccer in the field there," Mom said.

"Really?" I asked. But what I really meant was, "Really, I played soccer?"

• • • •

The Prince and Princess of Wales were formally divorced at court in London around the time my family decided to put me in first grade again. By "again," I mean a second year in first grade. There was a question of whether I belonged in school. The educational experts called this a "conditional placement." I had a condition all right, so this seemed fine to me. None of the experts knew for sure whether I would regain the skills I had lost, let alone learn new ones.

Back to the royalty, I loved Princess Di. My speech teacher looked just like her! It was decided that I would go to a mainstream school, not the special school for deaf children that I used to attend. Even that was confusing. *I'm not special anymore?* Did this mean I wasn't unique, wonderful, and desirable? Or did this mean I *didn't* have a problem? Ha! That was funny, the idea that I didn't have a problem. So I was going to the mainstream school, but I was in the worst shape ever. Go figure! Before the coma, when I was only deaf, I needed a handicapped placement. Now that I had no coordination, couldn't communicate, and had trouble thinking . . . suddenly I didn't need a special school?

For my second time in first grade, Mom took me to Eastview, a mainstream elementary right across the street from home.

"Remember coming to Eastview for Christmas craft shows, basketball games, and concerts?" my mom asked. "I always used names of people and places when I talked to you to help build your vocabulary."

Even though she tried, the frightening memory of walking into that unfamiliar place to join a class three times the size of any class I had ever been in is still with me.

My brain was waking up, and I had new memories and new fears. In room 104, a blonde-haired girl came up to me and said, "Hi, Lauren."

I was stiff, and I looked at her strangely. There was a sense of unfamiliarity, horror, and loneliness. Hugging my mom's leg for comfort and security, I wondered who she was. She looked nice, but how did she know me? Then it came to me—it must have been Abbi, the girl in the pictures that my speech teacher showed me—Abbi from South School. I whispered, "Hi, Abbi!" But this wasn't Abbi. She wasn't here at Eastview. My brain was not completely working yet. This girl knew my name because I was the only new kid, and Mrs. Dunn had told the class a deaf girl would be joining them.

"Mommy, who is she?" I mouthed instead of signing.

After all the therapy, all the medicine, all the time spent looking at pictures of myself playing with a blonde girl, and all the talk about a blonde girl named Abbi, here I was at a different school. Here I was, heading to the blue slide on the playground. Ideas and moments suddenly swirled in my head. Abbi was before the coma, and this blonde girl was not Abbi. Would the confusion ever stop? But wait, this was starting to make sense. This wasn't South, and this wasn't Abbi. I was getting it!

• • • •

I was six years old, and this was Mrs. Dunn's class. Her smile was so big that, sometimes, it would just make my day! No cakes with birthday names on the bulletin board in there. Raising my hand, kids said their names rather than signing them. Every day, I had to go home when the lunch bell rang. No one else went home. It was time to take my IV medicine that lasted for hours and felt like forever. This medicine was to cure my bacterial meningitis that had turned into encephalitis—to cure the thing that caused me to repeat first grade, even though I felt like I was in first grade for the first time. While writing and trying to think of how to spell in class, I raised my hand to ask about a word, and out of the corner of my eye, I saw someone fingerspelling the word. No kids signed at this school; they spoke. I don't remember what the exact word was, but I remember the feeling of having a connection to someone who understood me and being filled with happiness! The person who had fingerspelled the word was not my interpreter but a student! She had blonde hair, blue eyes, and was the type of student to be a teacher's pet and always get straight As.

Kelsi eventually introduced herself and asked why I called her Abbi a couple days earlier. Thoughts were running through my head that I thought they looked alike—for sure, they both had blonde hair and were pretty. I had to explain, "I don't remember calling you that, but Abbi is a friend from my past and you two look alike."

Kelsi was a little afraid to talk to me that first day because she didn't know if I would hear her. Despite this, she demanded that her mom take her to the library after school so she could get books about sign language. She taught herself how to fingerspell that very night. As much as she wanted to share her knowledge, she was afraid to fingerspell and make a mistake. So she kept her knowledge a secret at first.

Kelsi later told me she thought I was an angel when she met me. When she asked me very seriously about being an angel, all I could say was, "What are you talking about?" She thought I was an angel because of a story in the newspaper about me called "The Miracle Child, the Heart of Christmas." She read that I had two bad heart valves and needed a new heart to survive. In the article, it explained that doctors had put a new heart from a baby boy in me. She just didn't understand how someone could be alive with someone else's heart inside her. She asked me if it could fall out. Believe it or not, many people asked me that, but I knew it would stay right where it belonged because the doctors had sewn it in.

One day, Julie was at my house as usual for speech therapy. Trying to assess the level of my confusion, she showed me another picture of two girls. They were the same girls from the Aladdin picture, but in this one they wore blue scarves and were hugging. I was wearing a happy expression, and my arms were wrapped around Abbi's shoulders. Abbi was smiling as well, and it looked as if she was laughing along with me. I stared at the photo and felt some confidence return because I was able to recognize this *before the coma* friend. I answered, "She was my friend at South School."

When Julie heard this, she realized I didn't remember anything from before the coma, only after, and that pictures could jog old memories. To help me integrate my experience, Julie asked if she could invite Abbi to join our next speech session. Julie brought Abbi the very next week. The girl in the purple shirt came to life!

Every week was another week of learning about a best friend at Eastview, Kelsi, and another best friend from South, Abbi. As I got better, I was able to resume more playtime. By this time, I had re-learned how much fun it was to be with Abbi. I was glad to have the chance to practice signing. Even though I could read the signs, I was very slow at fingerspelling. Abbi was especially fond of my McDonald's French Fry Maker. We put slices of toasted bread through a crank, which came out in strips that we seasoned with cinnamon and sugar. We ate loaves of bread together, toasting, cranking, and sprinkling. We rebuilt our friendship. In my *after the coma* period, Abbi was my new friend and Kelsi was my old friend!

Some things were affected due to this "unexplained unconscious episode." I had a very hard time with math. Even though my father is a math teacher, I found that subject to be difficult. My parents told me my math skills had been damaged. The doctors suggested hypoxia, lack of oxygen to the brain. To make the best of the situation, I decided to become an artist because that's supposed to be the other side of the brain; maybe all the oxygen went to that side of the brain instead.

• • • •

Over the years, I often wondered why this amnesia happened to me. What would my life have been like if it hadn't happened, and I was a year ahead in school? What if I had never transferred to the mainstream school and had stayed in the program for the hearing impaired? There is no crystal ball that could tell what might have been.

Life has no guarantees, and there is no way to tell how things would be different. Would I be different? We are all shaped by our experiences, so I suppose so. I would be a different me.

Some things were affected due to this "unexplained unconscious episode." I'm very fortunate that my recovery was nearly complete and that my memory started to work again. As they said on the *Wonder Years*, "Memory is a way of holding onto the things you love, the things you are, the things you never want to lose." For me, the two friendships with Kelsi and Abbi, that I still have today, made the coma a positive thing for me.

12.
You Got Hit by What??

"Untitled" by Simple Plan and *"The House That Built Me"*
by Miranda Lambert

Before my brother knew it, I was old enough to drive. I took my
time getting my driver's license. From volunteering for Donate Life,
and hearing stories about car accidents, I was afraid to drive. Then,
eventually, the right time came around for me to get my license,
because I got a job at the library and I needed to be able to drive to
work. I think, partly due to caution because of my hearing loss, I
became a very cautious driver. I don't turn the music up too loud,
because I want to be able to hear an ambulance or squad car, if one
comes around. I depend on my visualization, and observe the drivers
around me to avoid any collisions. However, the first day I had my
license wasn't my lucky day, nor was it my brother's.

It was noon on an August day, the month to celebrate my Mom,
Dad, and Dave's birthday. I am the oddball, having a birthday in
December, instead of August with the rest of the gang. I was driving,
with my mother in the passenger seat, to the Division of Motor
Vehicles. I took the normal right turn from my street, a left, and then
headed off to the busy, accident-prone four-lane speedway known as
Randall Road. I crossed the bridge over the Fox River, not very far
from home. It felt just like a regular "permit" driving practice day,
except, today, I would be getting my license! I checked my mirror

to see the car behind me, as a normal driving caution. I kept driving down the road, toward the old downtown part of Algonquin.

My hands were both on the wheel, at seven and four rather than the ten and two positions they taught before airbags. The light turned red up ahead of me. I stopped, and would be the first car in my lane to proceed when the light changed back to green. I turned to look at my mom, to see what she was saying to me. As soon as I turned my head to look at my mom, her body was moving in an unexpected way and was a mirror reflection of what my body was doing at that exact second. Our shoulders were thrown forward, and my left shoulder hit the horn. At that time I felt a bump, and my neck was tapped in the seat belt. *Ouch!*

I looked quickly in my mirror to see the car behind me. It wasn't the same car that I had seen before, and certainly the driver wasn't the same person. It was my *brother*! That's right, my brother, David Aggen, had hit me! Mom was very calm, and told me to put my flashers on. Then she got out of the car, and saw that the car behind Dave hit him! It was a Jeep. My brother, the good guy he is, got out of the car to see if the person behind him was hurt. I was freaking out, and stayed in the car. This location is very busy, with another stoplight three car lengths ahead where two turn lanes are added. There was honking, and stares. I didn't like the attention, knowing the police would soon arrive. I kept asking my mom, "Is it my fault?" I knew it wasn't, but I was just scared. My brother checked on the lady in the Jeep. She said her leg was hurt, and she thought she had broken it. Getting out of the car, she faltered and walked hunched.

"This looks bad," I thought.

The woman asked Dave, "Why did that car stop?" Dave said, "That really doesn't matter. The car stopped, and I stopped, but you didn't."

The police and firemen were at my window before I knew it. When the police arrived, I got out of the car, and so did the lady who told Dave that she thought she broke her leg. I thought, "That's odd, because she is walking." By this time my Dad arrived and was checking to see whether anyone was injured. The paramedics wanted to take me to the hospital. "Compared to what I am used to, as far as medical situations," I said, "I am fine."

"Ma'am, are you sure? You may be in shock? How old are you?"

I said, "I am always pale, because I am immunosuppressed." I was very serious, because I was scared.

Then this friendly fireman, who was checking up on me, started chatting with my brother. Apparently they had gone to high school together. "Dave, we think your sister should get checked out. She is *very* pale, and she may have some internal injuries. She wasn't answering my questions."

Dave explained that with all the traffic noise it was difficult for me to understand because I am deaf. "The ghostly pallor is her normal color," Dave said, "and I talked with her. She is fine. Just scared."

In the meantime, the police took my permit, as my Mom took pictures of the damage on the three cars. Her car wasn't nearly as bad as Dave's. Mom's car needed a new bumper, but Dave's car needed attention to the front *and* back. I was glad that Dave and Mom were okay, but I'll admit that all I could think at that time was "Am I going to be in big trouble? Does this mean I can't get my license?" My mom and brother were trying to reassure me everything was going to be okay.

Dave thought something about the third driver was mysterious. She looked fine, but her comments didn't make sense. She changed her reason often. I looked across the street to the gas station where the officers were attending to the lady while an ambulance stood by. "Is that lady all right? Is she going to the hospital in the ambulance?"

"No," the officer replied. "Don't look so worried. That driver has been cited for a D.U.I. She's going to jail!"

I was shocked, because it was Saturday at noon, not late at night when you would think a drunk driver would be out driving.

There you have it: my brother and I were in our very first car accidents at the same time. Go figure! This event taught me a lot about responsibilities, and I am glad that everyone was okay, although Dave was the most bruised. I am thankful my family was with me for my first accident. My Dad drove over because he was very concerned about the fact that all three of us were in an accident. *He couldn't believe it!* I think my dad was the most frantic of us all, because he wasn't there. He didn't know all the details, until he saw the accident scene. He was happy to see all of us okay, but, after he knew that, he was worried about the cars. Dad drove all of us to the hospital, to get us checked out. Mom's shoulders and neck hurt. Same with me, but I actually had a huge bruise on my neck from the seat belt. My brother pulled a muscle in his shoulder and had a bruised knee. This was disappointing, because he was home to run in a marathon the next day!

Because the hospital was halfway to the drivers' license office, my family convinced me there was no reason to wait, that I *should* go to the DMV as planned. So I took my test. When asked, "Have you ever been involved in a vehicular crash?" I answered, "Yes, today! A drunk driver hit me on the way here."

"Well, that is a first," answered the examiner.

• • • •

For "Project Ignition," an award-winning service organization in my high school, I participated in organ donor awareness presentations. I was present for the demonstrations regarding the effects of driving drunk. Every year for prom, they have a day in which students see the results of a car crash out on the football field. They pick one or more students to dress and act as if they were in a prom night drunk-driving accident. Parents of students killed in such traumas read letters, expressing what they would say at the funeral. Everyone is very emotional, and students are reminded not to drink and drive. I'll never forget the one true story of a teenage girl who was hit by another car, and was trapped in her own car. The car burst into flames, and her body was burned, but she survived. I always think of her when the subject is car accidents. She is someone who I know suffers because of someone else's carelessness. She has to live with disfiguration. I think that story touched many others, as well as myself, and made us think about our driving.

We all need to help someone who is in an accident, and not to just stand there, doing nothing. In spite of this education, I was still surprised to be hit by a drunk driver. What if Dave or my mom had died in the crash? Lives can change in a blink of an eye. Be thankful for what you have every day.

• • • •

When someone needs a transplant, the transplant team must decide if people are good candidates. Will they understand what is expected of them to keep their transplanted organ functioning? Will they be compliant? Do they have a support system?

This has to be a very difficult observation, in my opinion, because transplant candidates can't control the people around them. They can't make their families or friends become supportive. My support system of family, friends, and community is awesome. My wish would be that everyone who needs a transplant has a group to surround him or her with love. We all need friends.

"You've Got a Friend," by James Taylor, reminds me of the time my brother sang that song as a soloist at his middle school concert. In a dark auditorium, with piano accompaniment, he wore these awesome black sunglasses. I often would clap out loud for him as a little girl, because I thought his voice was amazing! "Lauren," my parents would say, "please wait until he finishes singing!"

• • • •

I always tease my parents that my brother, Dave, is the perfect child. I know I'm their favorite daughter, and he is the favorite son.

"Davey, Davey, you're home!" My brother tells me when I was little, and he was attending high school, I could always make his bad day into a good one. I would run down the stairs, and jump on him before he could take off his backpack, to give him a hug, make him smile, or maybe give him a headache!

I used to always tell my parents that I wanted a sister, but I couldn't have asked for a better sibling than the one I have. Dave is seven years older than I am, and has never been afraid to act out the part of Prince Charming so I could be Snow White. On a cruise, we did karaoke together, and sang, "I Believe I Can Fly" by R. Kelly. In the hot sun, out on the promenade near the pool, where most of the guests were stretched out on the deck loungers, relaxing with colorful drinks, we both wore sharp looking sunglasses for fun. In the middle of the song, I stopped singing, and did the mime of singing. In my flowered bikini, I flapped my arms as if I were a bird, then stood on tiptoes and stretched to the sky. How Dave kept singing with my goofy antics is a testimony to his perseverance. He is the best brother in the whole world and my role model. In high school, Dave worked hard. He was valedictorian, an all-star athlete in cross-country and baseball, and sang in school musicals, but he could never color inside the lines like me! I have more creativity, but Dave is book smart, especially in science and math. I love my brother, and you wouldn't believe what a great all-around person he is! I admire him for always being nice to others and working hard in life to succeed. I never really liked school because of all the homework; I would miss so many days due to being sick. I was more into the school dances and clubs.

Coincidentally, my brother published a manuscript this year too! *Engineering Human Single-Chain T Cell Receptors* is 165 pages long, hard covered in black. My brother received his Doctor of Philosophy in Biochemistry in 2010, and is now attending medical school. I think after all the doctor appointments he went to with me, I played a part in getting him headed to where he is today, but he did all the work.

Dear Lauren,

Sometimes you go into a coffee shop, and you get a barista who is meticulous. The barista grinds the espresso beans and taps them to get the perfect grind and consistency, puts the espresso onto the machine, and delivers the perfect shot of caffeinated goodness. This type of barista isn't always the most outgoing or overly friendly, but they make a nice consistent cup of coffee in an efficient and timely manner. Other times, you go to the coffee shop and you get the eclectic and extremely friendly coffee maker. This type of barista is very interested in how your day is going (and potentially any baby names of your future children) and may need to ask for your order twice. The coffee may be too strong or too weak because special attention isn't paid to the process of making the coffee ideal, but that cup of coffee is made with an artistic interest in mind. The barista chooses the mug with the best pattern to suit you as a person, and possibly your mood on any given day. The swirl of milk with espresso is perfectly unique; it may not taste perfect, but this barista delivers the coffee with a smile and for that instant you are positively ecstatic to have obtained the most exquisite cup of coffee. If you haven't guessed it yet, Lauren, you are much more like the second coffee-maker. In fact, you probably can't stand the thought of the first type of barista, even though the barista is me, your older brother. It is through our differences that we have always shared a friendship, and grown to care for each other much more than most siblings.

Lauren, when you were born I was elated because all I wanted was someone with whom I could share the back seat. I was grateful after seven years to finally have a sibling around to fill that void. In fact, one of the first times I was able to share the car with you, on your trip home from the hospital for the first time, we were greeted by the media. You were deemed the miracle of Christmas and made the cover of the Chicago Tribune Magazine. *I think that initial experience give you some of the swagger you love to flaunt today. You reached quite the celebrity status with the local papers between bowling and your numerous scholarships.*

*   **To the Readers:** *As you will find out, Lauren has not had a typical road to turning twenty, but it has certainly been a most interesting journey.*

*   *Love to my special sister!*

Your brother,
Dave

13.
My Best Friend
"Come Away with Me" by Norah Jones

"Mom, not again," I cried. "You've played Norah Jones for about a million times. Every time we are in the car you play it over and over and over."

Mom replied, "It calms me."

"Can you *please* take the CD out? I am SOOOOOOOOOOOO *sick of it!*"

"I'll listen to my CD once, and then you can choose a CD for *one play!*"

• • • •

Okay, so I got a little tired of the song. However, when I went to college and had to go have an ultrasound for my leg by myself for the first time, and the song in the room was "Come Away With Me," by the *lovely* Norah Jones, I had a very different feeling about it! I felt as if my mother must have been with me in a sense. I didn't like going to the hospital alone with a problem. I missed having someone with me, even if it meant I would have to remember listening to Norah Jones in the car.

My mom is someone who I seriously think could be a doctor. After learning to take care of me, she knows all the medical terms and really knows how to take care of people. She's fun, has an outgoing personality, and is always shopping (for others, not herself). The worst thing my mother did when my brother and I were growing up was sing "Good Morning" when it was time to go to school. My brother and I moaned and groaned, but she kept singing it until we got up. How dreadful that song was! I got so annoyed with it.

• • • •

"Mom, *please*, can we just go home? You're always adding stops. I had a blood draw and I'm tired. Let's go *home!*"

When I was younger, after the *many* clinic visits, my Mom took excursions. She made an adventure out of the day. Growing up, sometimes I would complain because my mother liked taking me to new places, instead of just going straight home. Now, I realized she made my life fun! On the other hand, when I repeatedly had five to seven vials of blood drawn, I *was* tired. Alex, my friend who had a transplant just a month before me, her Mom (Annette), my mom, and I headed out after our 7 a.m. clinic visits and walked through Lincoln Park Zoo, or played at Oz Park, or went to Kohls' Children's Museum at opening time before it was crowded. We found Eli's cheesecake factory outlet, all sorts of playgrounds, and bakeries. Once Alex got rid of her feeding tube, we sampled restaurants and found favorites like "Mars" at Woodfield, Chevy's, Lang's, Russell's, and Cheesecake Factory.

• • • •

Whenever I missed school because I was sick, Mom made sure I caught up with my homework. She didn't want me to fall behind due to being immunosuppressed, so she made it a point to call in early and request the materials I missed—whether film strips or presentations— and she did her best to fill me in. But not in math—Dad forbade her to "teach" me anything related to math. I guess she has "old math" in her head, while Dad has up-to-date explanations that meet with the state standards.

When I went to college, she'd drive around Rochester, and occasionally got lost, but invariably she found some cute little boutique store to shop at. My mom is very optimistic like that. Unlike me, who might be a little worried about being lost, my mom has the confidence that reassures me everything will be fine. She uses her GPS, but likes to see the backroads. She always is open to trying new things, and especially places!

One recent memory of my mother that is pretty funny was flying home from New York to Illinois. I had a biopsy after taking finals, and she came along to make sure I would be able to get on the plane to go home for quarter break, because the anesthetic didn't always wear off quickly. Walking through security with our loaded carry-on bags, in the heightened security state, my luggage was pulled aside.

"Is this your suitcase?"

I was in la-la land, but I answered helpfully, "It's mine!"

Apparently, some suspicious items triggered their concern.

"You'll need to walk through that scanner."

There had been a lot of press about the safety of the new surveillance machines at airports. People were up in arms about the pat downs, which they were subjected to if they refused to go through the new scanners. I have had plenty of radiation due to all my check ups, and I didn't really want more radiation, but in my dreamy state I was very co-operative. The security guard told me to go through the body scanner, and I did. Nothing beeped.

Next, with gloved hands, they carefully unzipped my bag.

"There is an amaryllis bulb in there," volunteered my mom.

They pulled out the 20-centimeter prize bulb, and took it and the bag back to the X-ray machine.

The bag returned to the inspection area as the security people shook their heads.

"There is a pomegranate too," volunteered my mom. We had searched through the whole stack at the grocery store to find a 1-pound 6-ounce fruit.

The men gave my mom a blank stare, and pulled out the huge red globe.

The luggage returned and the guards were once again shaking their heads. I remembered there were two huge artichokes as well, but I said nothing because I figured they would find these shortly.

Finally, the luggage was no longer tying up the line, and apparently no longer looked like a bomb threat. My mother, who sometimes

My family!

doesn't stop talking, kept telling the security guard that we got this produce from Wegmans' because it was so much better than what we could find in Illinois.

"Ma'am, it wasn't just the produce; it was the hunting license here in the top compartment."

"Hunting license?" questioned my mom. "No one in our home hunts.

"That color alerted us; the neon green."

It was Dad's fishing license that he must have packed for an overnight to Lake Geneva. We were flying home for Thanksgiving at my brother's, and I wanted to bring some cool things from Rochester, New York. The flower bulbs were for my aunt, who would be picking us up at the airport in Illinois, and we wanted to give her a thank-you gift. These suspicious items and a fishing license delayed our departure.

When we got home, Dad asked, "How was the flight?"

Mom simply answered, "Security is tight."

14.

Father of the Bride

"My Girl" by the Temptations and *"Rock around the Clock"* by Bill Haley & the Comets

According to the personality-analysis drawing I did in my psychology class, I am most like my Dad. He's the reason I have awesome goals in life! My dad, Dave, is the type of father that any girl would be lucky to have. He would take time to explain the little things in life. For example, usually before or after a wedding, I would ask my father, "Does the bride stand on the left or right side of her daddy when they are walking down the aisle for him to give her away?"

As always, he would answer, "What if I don't want to give you away?"

I would laugh so hard after he said that. I thought that joke was the funniest thing in the world. "Dad, I'm only seven!" Gently, my dad would explain the answer. He would take hold of my hand and make my arm wrap around his. Then we would practice walking together.

Because of my father, I fell in love with the movie *Father of the Bride*. I felt that my dad was soft hearted, like Steve Martin's character. He looks so much like Steve too! Their eyes, lips, and face structure are the same. However, when my dad is sleeping, then he really looks like George Banks! Like George, Dad has a tendency to worry quite a bit, but he is always there for you.

My dad sat next to me on the couch and shared homemade popcorn when we watched movies. My Dad is king of the remote, and I loved it when he would fast-forward through the scary part of my favorite movie, *Snow White and the Seven Dwarfs*. I was afraid of the part where the princess ran through the scary woods to get away from the evil queen. Eventually, Dad would push play, and a beautiful cottage would appear on the TV screen. Oh, how I loved the warm, welcoming cottage in the woods! After viewing the cottage, I couldn't wait to see Dopey!

My dad carried me on his strong shoulders, in more ways than one!

During my life, I've learned that my dad is the most caring person I've ever known. Even though he can be stressed sometimes from work, he will always show you that he cares for you in special ways. He always left very early for work—he is a morning man. He would leave letters of encouragement for me on my towel so that, when I was getting ready for school, I could read them. He would mention the good things I had done, or encourage me to feel good about an upcoming test. He was a math teacher at York High School.

I don't quite know why anyone would want to teach math—it's so complicated! He was also a football and baseball coach. Surprisingly, he never played football in his life! Can you believe it? York won conference championships many times and even went to the state play-offs. He worked very hard to help his students succeed.

Even though my dad is a very big sports fan, he never drank beer while watching a game on TV. I have to say, I admire that! He never really drank unless he was at a wedding or took a sip of my kiddie cocktail. My dad made the best kiddie cocktails (and ribs too!). He always put two cherries in the kiddie cocktail because he knew that's the way I liked it.

My favorite thing to do with my dad is dancing with him during father-daughter types of songs at weddings. For my wedding, we're going to dance to a cool re-mix that I made. I think slow dancing can be boring, and re-mixes are fun to dance to! My dad and I have the attitude and skills for cool re-mix songs.

Dad always supported me at dance recitals. He would say something like, "How do you do that one step in that jazz dance? I thought it was really cool." Then, he would try to demonstrate what he was talking about.

• • • •

Now you have met my intermediate—oops, immediate—family (mix-ups like these happen often with the hearing impaired), I thought you should get to know them better before you read the next chapters, and understand that I am very close to my family. I am so glad that I lived to grow up in a family that is proud to connect with each other and that understands what the word "family" means. I know I couldn't have asked for a better set. My family isn't perfect, but I appreciate them and everything they've been through for me.

Thinking about my support system, I recognize that different people give different types of support. I haven't always said thank you enough to my many supporters: to my Church family, who cheers me on and keeps me in their prayers; for family that I might not acknowledge enough because they are there when I need them to be without even asking and don't expect accolades; to all the doctors and nurses and hospital staff that spent years training to give me the quality care I receive; to the teachers who took extra time to get me notes that were almost as good as closed captioning; and to my friends who understood sometimes I needed a little fantasy to get through tough times. Your support system doesn't have to be just like mine—but I sure hope you have one!

. . . .

We are family..... THE BIONIC FAMILY.

When my parents got married, and for the next 15 years, everyone was pretty much healthy and mostly happy. No one could have guessed that, hours after their daughter's birth, they would be considering a heart transplant for their seven-pound bundle of joy. However, my wait for a new heart was actually short, and there was hardly time to absorb the concept. Everyone got busy with tasks at hand, and we, for the most part, believed this unique experience wouldn't be repeated in our family. Life continued to surprise us, and, via my Grandma Aggen, we learned about the Illinois Eye Bank, after she was fortunate to receive a cornea transplant. She was overjoyed when she passed her driving test afterwards! We were doubly blessed. This wasn't to be our last connection with transplantation. My Uncle Dan, who lived with diabetes since his teen years, received a pancreas and kidney in a transplant operation ten years ago. With his life-saving operation, he not only avoided dialysis, he no longer needed insulin! So we are a bionic family because I am not the only person in my family to have a transplant.

My Uncle Dan is an amazing, inspiring man, and I have loved meeting up with him at transplant functions and organ donor awareness activities. He suggested the three of us pose for a picture— three generations of transplants! My Uncle Dan has quite the sense of humor, and you have to be paying attention or he can fool you! Whenever we are at a loud and crowded family event, he always says to me, "I'll do your hearing, and you can do my seeing!" I'd always laugh and appreciated the help. He has vision problems even with glasses on, and I have hearing problems, even with my hearing aids on.

One of my favorite memories of Uncle Dan was at my cousin's wedding. There was a huge crowd singing at karaoke, and *all* of the Aggen boys united, singing, "The House of the Rising Sun."

Uncle Dan's sons, Danny and Mark, were acting out the role quite dramatically, pretending to strum and play assorted musical instruments as they sang. My Uncle Dan's voice was really good, and he sounded like he belonged in a rock band. I wonder if he ever wanted to be a performer! I was so impressed, and it reminded me that people are filled with secrets and surprises. Uncle Dan can surprise you with his quick wit, and have everybody laughing out loud! This is particularly impressive in view of the fact that Uncle Dan has not had an easy road lately. He has had some complications that have sent him back for leg bypass and heart bypass surgeries. Last year he got a nasty infection, and it was really hard to shake. So the fact that he can be optimistic, encouraging, and downright funny is amazing to me. One day I had a clinic visit at the same hospital where he was

Three generations of transplants: Guess who has had one the longest! Uncle Dan (new kidney/pancreas, 1999), Grandma Aggen (new cornea, 1998), and me (new heart, 1989).

recuperating after surgery. I couldn't really go in his room to say hi, because I had a cold and didn't want to pass it on to him, knowing he is immunosuppressed like me! My mom went in to give him a bag of goodies, including a box of candy canes for the nice nurses only, while I quietly waited outside of the room, with a mask on, watching old people walking past me with their gowns slipping open in the back. Remember, I have to go to an adult hospital now that I am over 18, and most of the time the gowns are enormous on me, but somehow the small gowns seem to show up in the wing where some larger sizes are needed. Then suddenly I hear Uncle Dan shout my name! My mom signed to me across the room, what Uncle Dan was saying to me. Uncle Dan wanted me to come in to say hi, but my mother said I could only peek in for a minute. I made sure I had the mask tightly bound, and, knowing I had been on antibiotics for 24 hours, I peeked in quickly to wave hi. Just as I glanced in, he dramatically flopped back and let his head drop. His arms dropped off the bed, and, as my eyes opened in scared shock, he laughed and popped back up again to say hi. I can see where Danny and Mark get their comedian personalities!

Uncle Dan discussed our top three pieces of advice to other transplant patients:

1. Always take your medicine on time.
2. Get involved with organ donor awareness programs; you'll meet wonderful people, and it's fun!
3. Speak positively when in the company of others who have transplants.

Great advice, Uncle Dan!

After Uncle Dan's last stay in the "hotel," as I like to call the hospital, he was going to be released on the day of the Chicago Marathon. Uncle Dan ran in that race years ago, and now his son Dan was to run!

Uncle Dan wasn't going to miss that—so, when he couldn't reach the family by phone, he borrowed money from a nurse, checked himself out, and headed for the starting line! I *love* his determination!

I can't really tell you what my Grandma's advice would be, because she passed away. However, I must say, she was a wonderful grandmother, and she made delicious milkshakes!

15.
Butterflies

"Somewhere over the Rainbow" by Judy Garland or Israel Kamakawiwo'ole

Do you like butterflies? Have you ever seen a monarch migration? It is a stunning sight! There are butterfly museums and butterfly kisses, but butterflies mean something entirely different to me. They come in different colors, and I prefer blue because they are the smallest. I am talking about the needle the phlebotomist uses when drawing blood—you know, to check the level of your anti-rejection drugs, your kidneys, and about a thousand minerals, vitamins, platelets, red blood cells, lymphocytes, etc. The needle has a wing on each side, which allows the phlebotomist to hold the wings and have more control over the needle.

If you have regular checkups, as I do, you get to know the lab people pretty well. I actually feel sorry for people who have to stick babies for blood tests. I feel sorrier for the kids. The good news is that the pain is short-lived. Throughout my childhood, we tried various things to minimize the pain, such as drinking a lot the night before. However, the best plan is getting a phlebotomist with the magic touch—the one who has you laughing, and you don't even know you've been stuck. How do they do that? Is it their confidence, or do they have confidence because they are so successful?

Many of my days were spent in a medical setting, which influenced my playtime. I always searched Toys R Us and toy catalogs for medical paraphernalia—doctors' and nurses' kits and scrubs. Of course, my blood pressure cuff and stethoscope were real, because I used those every day. I even sent my American Girl doll to the hospital to get the doll hospital gown. For Christmas one year, my uncle gave me a wheelchair especially made for my doll. I even played with LEGO dentist and doctor sets! Anything the nurses were going to throw away after a checkup—oxygen masks, alcohol pads, bandages, or IV tubing—would be good equipment for my American Girl dolls. Naturally, we had to keep my IV pole for my doll nursery. Walking into our family room might have seemed gruesome to some of our guests. All of my dolls were receiving some type of treatment, and they frequently had bandages, tubes, and NG tubing taped to their mouths, just like I had done to me when I was a baby.

One year, my brother gave me a doll for my birthday. He saw me playing with her the next day. "The doll had marks from many different colored markers on her face, a tube taped to her mouth, an

Doctoring one of my dolls.

As a butterfly at Halloween.

IV tube taped on her arm, and a tube in her nose," Dave recalls. "I couldn't help but laugh!"

When I would have a friend over, we wouldn't play house. Instead, we would play doctor and patient. So used to being a patient myself, I was always the doctor because I truly knew how to give treatments to sick patients. Based on my experience, here is some advice for comfort during a blood draw:

1. Make sure you drink bottles of water or anything that does not contain fizz or caffeine the night before your appointment. Your blood will flow faster, and it will be over sooner! This makes the phlebotomist's job easier as well!

2. Be sure to drink after the blood draws so you don't become too weak from loss of blood.

3. Do not take any additional medication unless your doctor says it is okay. If you are taking a child to get his or her blood drawn, stay positive and supportive. When the child is going to get blood drawn, tell him or her a story or ask a question to distract the child from watching the needle go in. Something that worked for me was a stuffed animal. There was a huge Mickey Mouse on the table across from where I sat. I would just stare at it as the lady put the needle in. It helped that I loved Disney characters!

4. After going to the hospital for a checkup, labs, or a blood draw, my family would take me to the playground inside Oz Park. I loved going down the slides and having my dad or mom at the end of the ride to catch me. However, nothing made me as happy as going on the swings. I loved it when my brother would act as if I had knocked him down when I touched my feet to his hands, which were raised high over his head. It made me laugh, and that was what I needed most after a hard day at the clinic. To this day, I still love the swings. I have always loved the movie *Wizard of Oz*. At Oz Park, I was always greeted at the entrance by a huge, brilliantly shiny statue of my favorite character from the movie, the Tin Man. When I was little, I thought the Tin Man was real, and that he wasn't moving because his oil tank was empty. I felt like he knew me because he had a heart problem too. Remember, I was a kid with an active imagination—one who needed to escape from the unpleasantness of hospital visits.

16.
Mark

"He's a Pirate" (from *Pirates of the Caribbean: The Curse of the Black Pearl*) by Klaus Badelt

If I had to pick one person my age who brought adventures and positivity to my life, it would have to be my cousin, Mark. We were born seven months and twenty-five days apart.

Summer of 2002

I was twelve, and Mark was almost twelve. We were at Six Flags, an amusement park in Gurnee, Illinois. We saw a huge waterlog ride too appealing to pass up, but my mother wanted to take a break from rides.

"Go ahead, and I'll be sitting on this bench waiting for you to come off the ride," my mother said.

Off we went; I followed Mark's tow-haired head that was three inches higher than mine. We walked through the metal maze of lines quite quickly, because not many people wanted to go on a water ride on a cloudy day.

Mark, pumped with enthusiasm, turned to me and said, "Lauren, are you ready? Are you ready? Oh no, here's the big drop!" I was grabbing his shirt, creating a wrinkle or two. And then, after we went on a wimpy little bump, he smiled and said, "Just kidding! Ha ha ha, I got you!"

"Mark, you lied!" I shouted, unsure whether I should show a silly or angry face. I couldn't help laughing my head off.

After a few more seconds, he started up again.

"Lauren, oh no, this is it!"

But I didn't believe him because I thought he was joking again. I knew we were going up a long ramp, but I figured it would be another little bump with more mazes of turns at the top. I closed my eyes, though, just in case.

"Lauren, open your eyes and put your hands up," Mark said. Then he sang, "Put your hands up, put your hands up, it's your birthday." (You know that song, right?)

Just when we were about to tip and drop, I opened my eyes . . .

"AHHHHHHHHHHHHHHHHHHHHHHH!"

Even though I should have been sitting in front of him because I weighed less, I insisted on sitting behind him so I could wrap my arms around him and feel safe. Otherwise, I was afraid I would fall out.

We left the ride and walked toward the bench where Mom had told us to meet her. Surprise! She wasn't there. It was just like all the times I had to try to find my mother in a grocery store. We walked around the park two or three times, and then Mark came up with a smart plan. We went to the first aid office, and two officers joined us as we walked around the park trying to find my mom. Mark did all the talking because he was calm and cool. I was frantic, but Mark assured me that everything would be fine.

I couldn't believe it; my mom was sitting on the bench! The officers looked at Mark and me as if we were dumb. I looked at my mom, feeling very angry, but Mark was laughing. My mother had left to buy something at the store for my cousin and me. I rolled my eyes.

I credit Mark with teaching me to let go; to realize that I didn't need to hold on to the safety bar. Mark helped me to feel the thrill of roller coasters. Six Flags isn't the only adventure we've had together. In fact, my many little experiences with Mark when I was young were just preparing me for a big adventure.

Family Get-Together

I'm at the end of the twenty-four cousins, but at the beginning of the ten second cousins. I am always excited to see my little cousins, and I play with them during family events. I love holding baby Talon, but I know she doesn't like me holding her for a long period of time. At a recent get-together, after she had just learned how to walk, she started to squirm her way out of my arms. She was enjoying the freedom of her new accomplishment, in awe of her success at walking on carpet. However, when Mark came through the front door, it was a whole new story. All the little ones started jumping on him; they didn't seem to mind when he held them. There always seem to be babies and toddlers growing up in our family. I can't blame the little ones, because Mark is fun to be around. He is a comedian, a talented musician, and a really good athlete. He is really tall, at least a foot taller than me. I think it's cool that he can play "Bad Day" on the piano and sing it too!

Mark is very good at talking to Koralyn and Jake. Mark wrestles with Jake and asks him how school is going. He is sort of like the big brother Jake never had and someone I'm sure Jake looks up to. Koralyn is comfortable enough to talk to Mark because she trusts him. Mark is the cousin who makes her laugh, takes time to play volleyball with her, or even take her out for lunch. In turn, Koralyn was the one to shave Mark's hair for the summer. However, she began with a Mohawk!

I'm happy that Mark is my cousin, and I think he's one of the coolest people ever! I think it would be great if Mark grew up to be a teacher. He's so good, patient, and caring with everybody. It's no secret that, all the time we were growing up, I wanted my best friend Kelsi to marry Mark so that Kelsi and I would be related, and I could hang out with Mark more too.

High School

Throughout high school, Mark and I went to each other's events. Whether it was a play, a bowling meet, a volleyball game, or a musical, I loved going to cheer for my cuz! Mark always seems to be so popular. So many girls go up to him and talk. In school plays, he usually had a big role because he was a boy with many talents. Mark was very outgoing in high school, whereas I was shy. He always says, "Lauren, go out and meet people. It won't hurt!"

When I first met his friends, everyone called him "Mark Davis," not just Mark. I figured he was really popular because everyone called him by two names!

I have to say that my cousin—"Mark Davis"—is a phenomenal person. And to the girl who ditched my cousin at the last minute on prom night: *your loss*! (I know she was sorry later because she snuck away from her date and had her picture taken with Mark—she sent the photo to him with a heart on the back.) Instead, Mark had a very good date with another girl who was very pretty, much nicer, and more humble than the princess who ditched him for another guy. And Mark is a very good dancer. I have witnessed it at family weddings!

Things Mark and I have in common despite our opposite personalities:
1. We both love cheese (his with bacon, and mine with Sun Chips).
2. We love entertaining!
3. We are the two grandchildren who never met our Grandpa Aggen (he died three months before I was born).
4. We like to play cards.

Things that Mark and I have in common because he taught me to love them:
1. Roller coasters
2. Trying out for a play
3. Bowling
4. Golfing
5. Jumping off a cliff in Hawaii
6. Trying out cool tricks on the trampoline
7. Doing a back flip in the pool
8. Learning to love dogs
9. Rules for basketball games

And best of all . . .
10. He helped me make my "bad-flavored" smoothies. We wanted to make a delicious drink for all to enjoy; his recipe saved the family party.

17.
Biopsies
"Who Knew" by Pink

What does a biopsy mean to me? I get one every year. It's a time to check and see if my heart is in any stage of acute or chronic rejection. I always look forward to the cool music that Dr. Wax plays on his iPod speakers. Dr. Wax, with his dry sense of humor, kind ways, and bald head, is great. He had been on call one night when I came in through the ER. I had been making brownies in jars to sell for a church fundraiser. Unfortunately, as I bent over the jars to fill them, I inhaled too much cocoa powder dust and my lungs began to swell until I couldn't breathe. I was rushed to the ER and, after testing, Dr. Wax proclaimed that I was indeed suffering from brownie dust ingestion. He said he could see the powder right there in my chest! What a tease!

At Children's, there were butterflies and clouds on the ceiling that I watched as consciousness drifted away after the anesthesiologist began his magic. Oh, how I love music! The music helped distract me from the fear, and soon I was dreaming about my future or something positive. First, I would get an IV. Before the procedure, I always got a black marker from my coloring box and drew a huge black X on my left hand and arm. I didn't want the IV to be inserted in my left hand because that's the hand I write with. I wanted to color after the surgery, and it was easier for me to color with the hand I write with.

Eventually, the nurse would see the X and put the IV in my right hand. I got that awesome drug that made me feel like I was flying on cloud nine. I tended to tell the truth while I was on it, which could be a bad thing or a good thing. I dreamed about the beautiful kiddie design on the ceiling, with rabbits, trees, clouds, and the unique shade of blue sky, as I quickly drifted off to sleep. Then the doctor did his thing, and I woke up in ICU. I usually woke up without hearing aids in my ears, because I usually took them out before surgery so they wouldn't get lost. When a nurse would come up to check my status, is sounded like "H mom dad. H yo fee," which was very unclear to me. This was not only because I didn't have my hearing aids, but also because the anesthetic was not completely out of my system yet. Luckily, I could read lips and figure out what the nurse was asking.

After an hour, I would be released to the cardiology unit on the fifth floor. The nurses pushed my bed to my new recovery room. I was always in a single room alone because I required isolation, due to my immunosuppression. I was aware that I had to stay in a prone position for eight hours, lying completely flat on the hospital bed. I couldn't even have a pillow to support my head because I wasn't allowed to move my neck. I couldn't move my legs either. This was because the doctors put a needle through my groin going up into my heart. I had a huge bandage on my neck, because they accessed my heart in both places, and I felt sort of like a mummy being taped down.

However, eight hours wasn't that bad for me. The nurses gave me a drink whenever I wanted; cute little cans of lemon-lime that were absolutely delicious! Because I couldn't lift my head to drink out of a can, my parents or Dave would squirt the liquid into my mouth with a syringe. I could also use a straw, which was a favorite way of mine when my Aunt Donna would help me drink.

My family always made the eight hours fun for me with sticker books and velvet coloring projects. Looking back, I realized my family really tried hard not to disappoint me. They were always there to support me; they are still making that same effort.

Even though it was hard for me to color in the air, my mom would help by holding the coloring book for me. Eventually, I would get tired and watch a movie of my choosing with my family. I would pick a movie that was sure to put my dad to sleep, because I figured he needed his rest. I would happily watch a fairy tale story such as *Snow White and the Seven Dwarfs*.

I don't mean to make this sound like everything was perfect, but I want to show how much I appreciate having the family I do. Keep in mind, if something unique was going to happen to someone, it would usually happen to me!

I had my good and bad biopsies. Good was when the day went by fast, and I wasn't in too much pain. Bad was when I had my period the exact same day as the surgery. I didn't care to take my underwear off for the surgery (which was customary) and start bleeding on the table. I'm sorry if I caused any of the men who were operating on me to lose their man card. It was the cramps that bothered me, and knowing that the nurses had to change my bed pad because there was so much blood. I felt like an invalid!

I will never forget the *worst* (and very recent) biopsy of my life in June 2008. However, there was a happy ending.

It was a Monday, as I recall. The previous Friday, I had gone to the prom with a guy I thought I loved. But, hey, he was my first love—I was suffering through the teen years the same as everyone else.

His name was Andrew. He was Italian, and his birthday was on the twenty-second like mine, but in July rather than December. We were at the movies, and, right before the movie started, he turned and looked into my eyes and said, "I had an amazing time with you at prom, but I don't want to lose you. I think it's best if we just stay friends."

As he was trying to break up with me, I was blacking out because my body was shutting down. Andrew saw my pale face as I collapsed into the empty movie seat on my left.

Due to the blackout, the doctors wanted to do a biopsy on me, but not at Children's. *I was seventeen*; therefore, they transferred me to an adult hospital in Chicago. I knew it would be different—no touchy-feely personnel, no colorful decorations, and no Nintendo to pass the time. The bleak beige surroundings certainly didn't help my disposition in the midst of discomfort and fear.

This would be the worst of all my hospital experiences. I was put to sleep, but there were no rabbits, trees, or friendly blue skies for me to gaze at as I drifted off. The ceiling was white. That's it! I felt very negative about going to sleep. I missed Dr. Wax's music. (The last song he had played for me was "Who Knew" by Pink.) As I went to sleep, I thought, "Who knew this would happen to me? Being a patient in a depressing hospital!"

I woke up without any bandages. I was shocked. I vaguely remembered the nurses pressing on my leg to stop the bleeding. It was like a dream, but that was about the time the drug that makes me feel like I'm flying high was wearing off.

I kept complaining of pain, as I had never felt this awful after a biopsy. Plus, my room made me feel sad because it looked as if I was in a rehab room. The walls were completely white, a sharp contrast from Children's colorful walls. And there was no TV! The recovery room was a sterile environment with glass walls and a bland curtain that, when staff remembered, could be pulled across the room for privacy. At Children's, we had our own bathroom! Here, the commode was right out in the open. I felt sorry for all the adults who had to endure this humiliating treatment. I wanted out of this place!

After observation, the doctor who operated on me (not Dr. Wax) decided some additional study was needed, and a different team was called in. When the doctors looked at my results, they had no conclusion. They felt there was a possibility some nerves had regenerated from the donor heart and were competing with the nerve impulses of my heart. However, an obstruction forced them to stop, and they decided to look into it at a later time.

I was sent home in the worst pain of my life. After only a few hours at home, my mom took me to my fabulous, gifted, energy-filled, excellent diagnostician and pediatrician, Dr. Brown, who recommended an ultrasound. I looked so bad that she wouldn't even let Mom take me the one block to the hospital; instead, she called an ambulance!

It turns out that I had a hematoma that was thirteen centimeters long and one centimeter wide. Apparently, a nick created this bleed. Because blood is an irritant, all my neighboring organs were distressed. I was put on a morphine drip after being transported back to the city hospital.

Most high school students would say that junior year is the hardest. I agree. I was lying in the hospital bed thinking about my awful breakup, how much schoolwork I would have to do to complete junior year (especially math, which was torture for me), and all those finals!

Some good news came along while I was recovering—news that motivated me to want to get out of the hospital. The National Institute for the Deaf at Rochester Institute of Technology (RIT) had called to let us know that I won their "SpiRIT" writing contest. I would get to participate in a two-week program at RIT called Explore Your Future (EYF) that would show me what college life was like and help me figure out what major was right for me. They would pay for both my mom and me to fly to Rochester, New York, on July 19. While I stayed in a dorm, she would stay in a hotel. I had only three weeks to get in shape!

In my head, I needed to get better by July 19. But blood takes its own time to absorb. The pain management was morphine, oral after the drip, which allowed me to go home. However, it took me a whole month to get out of the hospital. I was so miserable. For the first time in my life, I yelled a lot and began to swear! My mother said I was acting like a different person. Though patient, this experience stretched all of my family members to the limits because the drugs had me acting very weirdly. To heal the hematoma, I had to walk. From my first step, I was in the worst pain of my life. Slowly it started to improve, but my days were like a horrible rollercoaster. Some days, the nurses forgot to bring my medicine or gave me the wrong dose. My mother was a smart woman and knew what I needed to take. I couldn't really stand up for what I needed, because I was so out of it from the morphine. Over my mother's objections, I was given double doses and then more drugs to counteract the overdose. I never got any food due to some mix-up in the cafeteria.

When I got out of the hospital, I did finish my junior year schoolwork and finals to get promoted to senior year. As I was doing that, I grew stronger and began volunteering at Safety Town. I had rough days when I couldn't do anything and thought about giving up and not going to EYF. I just didn't think I could physically participate in activities of any kind, let alone travel five states away. However, my family encouraged me to go, and the rewards for making it to EYF were three-fold:

1. I felt a little bit more like myself once I met new friends.
2. I found that RIT was the university I wanted to attend in the fall of 2009.
3. I met someone who enjoyed my company, and whom I enjoyed getting to know. Plus, he was really good-looking (despite being a little too tall and not having blue eyes).

18.
Inner Beauty

"Beautiful" by Christina Aguilera

Do you remember the age when you were waiting to lose a tooth so you could put it under your pillow for the tooth fairy? The tooth fairy would leave a surprise, maybe money or a coloring book or a toothbrush? I remember when my first tooth became loose. I brushed more often and used lots of toothpaste trying to get the tooth bright white so the tooth fairy would take it away. I didn't want the tooth fairy to say, "What an ugly yellow tooth! Throw it in a dumpster, and let's get out of here!" I wanted my tooth to go to the tooth fairy palace, a place that I pictured from a book I had read. According to the story, my name would be engraved on it.

I have always hated going to the dentist. I can't relate to my friends when one of them says, "It feels so good to have my teeth cleaned." They say this as they smile with their perfect, beautiful, white teeth.

On my trips to the dentist, the dental hygienist (or "hygician," as I called them) would tell me to brush and then chew a tablet that left red gunk on my teeth, supposedly indicating the places I missed when brushing. After obediently scrubbing with the cheap toothbrush, red stains remained all over my teeth, even though I had been brushing my teeth daily! The dental hygienist, always with a gorgeous white smile, would instruct me, "You need to brush more. Do you see the red over here and over there? Let me show you the proper way to brush."

It made me want to cry. Due to the medicine I have to take, I have yellow teeth and gums that grow over them. I'm not happy about it. I would love to have beautiful teeth when I smile. Telling me I don't brush enough or the right way doesn't help. Don't blame me for something I can't control!

On a side note, the most amazing thing is that my brother, who has never been one to drink soda or eat candy and desserts, has more cavities than I could have in a lifetime. He had five caps before kindergarten!

The only relief came at the conclusion of the visit, when I walked away from the pale seat to get a bag of goodies—dental floss, a new toothbrush, and my choice of stickers.

Orthodontist

I had my excess gums removed from my teeth at the age of twelve—a gingivectomy. Tissue was growing down and covering my teeth, due to the anti-rejection medicine I was taking at that time. I looked as if I had no teeth because the gums almost covered my incisors. The dentist kept telling me I wasn't brushing enough. Why do adults pass the obvious and blame everything on kids? Mixed with orange juice, the special medicine, called Cyclosporine, had side effects including excessive hair growth, hyperplasia (excessive gum growth), and kidney damage. I learned at a young age that Cyclosporine is made from a special mushroom that grows in a forest in Switzerland. Maybe that is why it costs more than $200 a bottle! This medicine would be squirted into my mouth, using a syringe, three times a day to prevent my body from rejecting my new heart. As a kid, I was allowed to stay up till midnight for the final dose of medicine. I felt so cool, because most of my friends had to go to bed before ten o'clock on a school night!

Near my twelfth birthday, I was scheduled to have my braces removed for the second time. I had to wear a pink, glittery permanent retainer in my mouth. At this point, I begin to catch on that my teeth would never be normal. The surgery I needed to fix my jaw is too major, and I would not heal from it due to the anti-rejection medication. I wanted pretty white teeth like those models in the magazines; I still do. A second undesirable side effect of the drugs is discoloration of the teeth, a kind of yellowish-white. I looked like a seven-year-old with the kind of teeth I had. When I smile and close my lips, I look twelve. But if I laugh or smile in excitement, I'm back to looking like I belong in the first grade due to my teeth being covered by gum tissue. I was insecure, and it can still affect me today. I am twenty, but I look fourteen.

Whenever I try out for plays, I always get the kid roles because I have the energy of a child. Also, it's because of my young looks, which I think is due to my teeth. In my experience, a director looking to cast an actress in the lead role usually selects a pretty girl, one with a beautiful smile and white teeth. I learned to accept that it's okay if I'm not the lead, and I guess I'll always play the kid role. However, I would like to play "Juliet" someday, and be the one to wear a beautiful outfit instead of a kid's clothes.

The orthodontist's office is a place where teens spend a lot of time. Perhaps that is why the offices now have hand-held games for kids to use while they wait. They give tokens for motivators, and have drawings to make your visit pleasant. But none of that helps when your mouth hurts.

"My palate expander hurts," I reported to the hygienist at the orthodontist's office.

"I can't see any reason for your discomfort. Sometimes the wire tightened on your teeth causes strain on the palate. You have been complaining for a while, but it needs to stay in until you have your gum surgery. That should be very soon. We'll take it off then."

Little did they know there was a big surprise growing under the retainer.

Finally the day arrived, and I was given general anesthetic to prepare for the gingivectomy. The gum surgery took longer than expected. Two specialists working as a team were expecting to cut the gums back from every tooth, with some areas requiring stitches. While I was under general anesthesia, the doctors first took out my retainer. Soon after, the surgeon rushed into the waiting room, where my supportive parents were drinking coffee and my Dad was doing a crossword in *The Daily Herald*.

"We've run into a complication," the surgeon informed my parents. "There was a tumor growing beneath the retainer. The pressure Lauren complained about was real, and probably much more severe than we could have imagined. It has a blood supply. We will work to remove it and cut off the blood supply. We will keep you posted, but this could take several hours."

See? I wasn't lying! I was in pain because a tumor had been growing underneath my retainer! It was like a huge gumball wedged between my retainer and my upper palate. By the time the doctors had it under control, all the skin had been removed to the bone on the roof of my mouth. At last, they could begin removing the excess gums. In total, the operation took more than twelve hours, with two surgeons working non-stop.

My body's response to the simple, common experience of wearing a retainer was devastating. The tissue had to be removed down to the bone. I had no skin on the top of my mouth. When I woke up, I discovered that I couldn't drink or eat until tissue grew back over my palate. The risk of infection was tremendous, so I was placed in isolation on the intensive care unit for two weeks, until I could drink fluid once again. After recovery, my gums started to grow back, because of the Cyclosporine. No matter how hard and often I scrubbed my teeth, this undesirable side effect would continue. I knew I might have to repeat this surgery again.

The third thing Cyclosporine affected was my appearance. I had lots of hair. In some places, thick hair is outstanding. My eyelashes, long and thick, made me look like I was wearing mascara. The hair on my head looked as if I was wearing a bunch of extensions. My curls were always bouncing, and the sheer volume of hair took forever to dry. On the other hand, the extra growth of hair on my face, arms, and stomach made me feel insecure. It sure didn't seem like peach fuzz as everyone kept trying to tell me. I felt like I belonged in the movie *Jumanji* in the role of a hairy monkey.

I am grateful that I have family and friends who love me for me. They didn't care whether I had too much or too little hair. I only felt insecure when I was sad about something in school. At those times, the extra hair, extra gums, trembling hands, and pale skin were sources of anxiety and self-doubt. Cyclosporine gave me a library full of side effects to pick from and feel sad about. My parents taught me to avoid those excuses because they wouldn't get me anywhere. And to this day, I agree.

As time passes, drug therapy changes. Cyclosporine was replaced, and the new drug has different side effects. No more hairy arms, face, or back. Now I need mascara! My new drug comes as a caplet and capsule. I no longer need to mix it with orange juice, so I don't have to carry syringes. However, I do have a large collection of shot glasses that are going unused.

When I look at pictures of myself growing up, I realize at certain times that I did feel insecure about my smile. However, I couldn't find a single picture where I wasn't showing off my gums. I was a very happy teenager who went through the normal periodic mood swings. I was involved in and out of school. I made my middle school pom-pom squad, went to state for my science fair project, and won scholarships for bowling tournaments. From this experience with my teeth, I have learned that inner beauty is what truly matters. Many people have liked me and didn't care about my teeth.

Sometimes, people ask if I have ever had braces before. I tell them that I did and then just walk on. Although, sometimes, I do think about what other people think of me, like when they ask, "Are you wearing braces?" I usually say, "No, I talk funny due to a hearing loss." That is a fact. Have I ever thought of having surgery on my teeth to make them perfect? Sure, but it's too expensive. I'd rather have a puppy.

Another challenging side effect of my anti-rejection medication was shaking. In high school, side effects from the drugs Cellcept and Prograf started interfering in some of the things I wanted to do. It started while I was signing to my interpreter, Mrs. Kern. I was talking to her outside of class when my hands suddenly stopped doing whatever sign I was putting in action. I felt a shock in my hands, and they froze up briefly. I was confused at what was happening. I just stared at Mrs. Kern and then continued signing, figuring it was something that wouldn't happen again.

Of course I was wrong, and it started happening more frequently. I noticed whenever I was playing a sport, or doing anything involving a lot of handwork, that my hands would shake. My handwriting went from bad to horrible! I talked to my parents about it, and they had noticed my hands shaking as well. I went to the doctor, who wanted to treat me for anxiety, but I wasn't nervous! My hands would just tremble for no reason.

The next day, I had to give a presentation in front of my class. Mrs. Johnson was one of my all-time favorite teachers. She was blonde, tanned, very pretty, and kind. She wore bright-colored, lovely fabrics and cute high heels. Well rehearsed, I was ready to give one of the five required speeches for the class. This first assignment was to read a book with expression. My classmates were dreading this assignment, but I volunteered to go first because I had chosen a book that I loved reading as a child.

Mrs. Johnson saw my hands trembling. Actually, she saw my papers shaking and thought I was very scared.

"Lauren, why don't we postpone your speech until tomorrow."

"Mrs. Johnson, I am ready, and I would like to do my speech today."

Most high school students dreaded public speaking. I thought it was fun and a chance to be creative.

"Take some time and look things over again tonight. I'm sure you will do well tomorrow." She was thinking I was nervous and more preparation time would help.

"I worked very hard on this presentation, and I am psyched today!"

"Well, as you wish, Lauren. Take the floor."

She allowed me to present, but then another problem arose when I stood in front of the class. I realized I had to read a book and show the illustrations with enthusiasm. Holding a book should not be of concern, but I realized they would get dizzy watching the book shake. I asked for a volunteer to hold the book. To save myself embarrassment, I explained to the class that my hands shook due to some medication.

After class, I thought about what I had said, and figured I had made myself sound like I must have some mental or nervous problems. Yet the class enjoyed my presentation because I was expressive in voice and facial expression, used humor and animation to keep their attention, read in different voices while adding in a few of my dramatic facial expressions and jokes. They laughed at my choice of material— *The Little Old Woman Who Was Not Afraid of Anything!*

The worst shaking situation occurred during a bowling meet. I was a starter for the first game, and, in the third frame, I lost control of the ball. Both hands were trembling, and I couldn't stop. It was difficult to hold my fingers in the holes of my twelve-pound purple ball with my shaking right hand. I tried my best, but it was something I couldn't control. I didn't bowl the rest of the day; it was a huge disappointment.

I returned to the prescribing cardiologist with my concerns, and I left her office with a prescription for a blood pressure medication that she felt might help. The severity of the shaking varied, and I wasn't wild about adding another drug to my daily regime. However, the offending drug was replaced, and I now enjoy stable hand movement. It *is* much better for sign language!

19.

My Tiger Bite Scar

"You Gotta Be" by Des'ree

You know how sometimes a kid's smile can just make your whole day? It's amazing how those little things can matter the most in life. That's how I feel about my little cousin Jake. He may only be a kid, but he said something that helped me overcome my insecurity about the surgeon's artwork on my stomach.

As I walked on the hot, wet, slippery pavement that bordered the pool, people were staring at my body. I knew exactly what they were looking at, and the reason they kept staring is because it was something they had never seen before. They were intrigued, wondering what happened to me. The eyes of a little girl scrunched up as in *ewww-that-thing-on-your-stomach-is-ugly*. A grandfather chasing his grandson slowed down as he saw my mark of bravery—and before he knew it, his grandson had fallen on the wet pavement and was crying. They ignored the fact I was wearing surfer bottoms that went down to my knees. My top was a Pacific blue color with two thin straps, like a bra with a halter-top. Even the guys around my age stared at the unique design on my body.

My friends from school think I look cute in a bikini. When people stare at my stomach, I feel like it's a sign showing that I am a fighter and tough at heart.

It is thirteen inches long and one inch wide. The line is pink, bumpy, and rough compared to the naturally pale skin around it.

When I look at it, the left side of the pink line is violet and partially blue, like a dented bruise. There are fifteen holes on each side of the line, for a total of thirty holes from the staples that were inserted to hold my skin together.

Dear Diary,

Today I got my period! I didn't like getting up and walking to the bathroom to change as the nurse changed my sheets that were full of my blood. Another nurse used rough, white washcloths to clean the blood off my legs. I had a male nurse today, and he was really nice about taking care of me, but I felt weird having a male cleaning up my girl stuff. I experienced an awful pain today. They pulled the tube out of the left side of my stomach—it was doing something to my body, but I am unsure of what. However, when the nurse pulled it out, I felt like I was shot with a bullet. I felt the air getting inside of me, and it hurt so badly! They told me I would have a circle-shaped scar from it, besides the big one on my stomach. I am tired from this exhausting day. I am going to watch Alice in Wonderland *with Dave. —Lauren*

I disliked having staples in my stomach! Why? Because I could see little openings here and there—it was disturbing! Until my scar could heal, I had to be careful. It was like I had metal rods holding me together, and, if the metal rods broke, I would be torn apart! I was afraid to do anything that would cause my stomach to get damaged. The feel of metal staples, one after another, across my own skin was disgusting.

The truth about my scar was that it was from the removal of my gall bladder and a choleductal cyst. I had vague abdominal pains that we thought might be related to menstrual cramps or indigestion. An ultrasound searching for a cause revealed a secret that was had probably been hidden since I was born. Unfortunately, I couldn't have the laparoscopic version, so I missed my confirmation because of the *big* surgery!

• • • •

I saw his smiling face, instantly setting him apart from all the others at the pool who found my stomach to be different.

"Lowen!" said Jake. He couldn't say my name completely right, but that was okay.

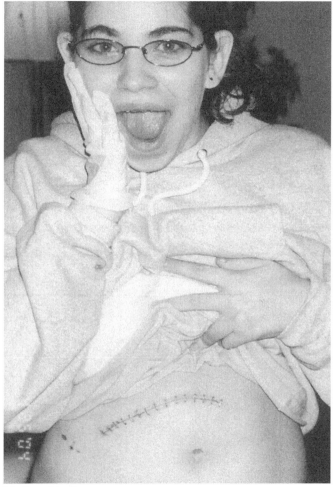

My "tiger bite."

"Are you ready to go swimming?" I asked excitedly.

He shouted, "Yes!" as he punched his hands up in the air like a superhero. (Hmmm, his bedroom is done in a Spiderman theme, now that I think about it.)

Unlike so many others, Jake happens to love my scar. The year before, all the Aggen cousins had gone for a swim in the community swimming pool, and he had asked me about the mark on my stomach.

"A tiger bit me, Jake." That was my answer—a lie—because I was so sick of people asking me that same old question over and over.

"Wow! You survived being attacked by a tiger! That's awesome! I'm gonna tell all my friends at school about your tiger bite," he said. He assumed the thirty holes were teeth marks from the tiger. Smart kid, I tell you.

After he said that, I laughed and realized he was right. I had survived something! Okay, a tiger hadn't exactly bitten me, but I was brave for what I went through. Plus, how often do you get to tell little kids that a tiger bit your stomach?

After swimming, Jake held my hand as we walked back to my house. (His mother told him he had to hold hands with someone while crossing the street.) Hyper as always, he kept asking me questions.

"Can I touch your tiger bite scar?"

"Sure, but be gentle," I said. Even today, my scar feels numb and sort of weird—kind of like the feeling when someone presses on your stomach, but you don't feel the pressure.

"Whoa! That is so cool!" He paused. "Lowen. Hey, Lowen?"

"Yes, Jake. What?"

"I think you're a brave person. Mommy tells me you're a brave cousin."

"Thanks, Jake."

Today, I'm glad I have a scar from my tiger bite.

20.
Hope You Think of
That Little Black Dress!
"Would You Go with Me" by Josh Turner

When I was sixteen, I remember running home and telling my mom that I had a boyfriend with benefits. My mom's reaction was "What!" I told her, "He has a big pool, a big house, and a big kitchen!" My mom was so relieved I didn't mean something else.

I am so happy he was my first love; he was one of my best friends. I know how important it is to have a powerful friendship beneath the romance. We were most definitely the "opposites attract" type of couple.

The Prince	*The Princess*
Birthday: July 22 (the hottest day of the year)	Birthday: December 22 (the coldest day of the year)
Brown eyes	Blue eyes
Tall	Short
Tanned skin	Pale skin
Loves to drive	Doesn't like to drive
Oldest in the family	Youngest in the family
Nice handwriting	Horrible handwriting

Doesn't like swimming	Loves swimming
Hates roller coasters	Loves roller coasters
Wants to be a cop	Firefighters!
Catholic	Protestant
Childhood favorite:	Childhood favorite:
Ghostbusters	Disney princesses

I enjoyed going out with a boyfriend, and we had a lot of fun together. His family was charming, and they knew how to have fun at a party. I could have lived in their pool, but Andrew wasn't as interested in swimming as I was. He volunteered in the community and was busy with a variety of service organizations.

Although we were busy with school and clubs, the one thing I always longed for was to be in a wedding. Having been to *many* cousins' weddings, I was patiently waiting for a turn to be a bridesmaid. Geoff and Annie had included me in their weddings by putting me in charge of the guest book. When I was finally asked to be a bridesmaid, I was elated! Christine honored me by asking me to go with her to shop for her wedding dress. The date of her wedding was my parents' anniversary too. As it happened, it was also the one-month anniversary of my dating. Walking out of the chapel, he surprised me with flowers, a card, and . . . paper? Of course! Don't you know that paper is the traditional one-month anniversary present? The flowers were blooming all around me, and it was the perfect temperature for a summer day. Between the wedding and my boyfriend, it was a very happy summer.

He was the best dancer I have ever met! It was so much fun! For homecoming, he wore his black shirt, and I wore my little black dress. It impressed me that he selected a corsage for me all on his own. Of course, it only took two seconds to tell the florist that I wanted a blue rose. I gave Andrew a red rose because I thought red would look good on him. That evening was wonderful! However, as is the case with many teens, a week later we broke up. He used the line; "I don't want to lose you as a friend." I knew what it was like to have a broken heart, but now I had experienced another kind of broken heart! Stresses were complicating our lives, and our relationship became a game of

Chutes and Ladders; we'd be progressing and then drop to the starting line again. I didn't even know what the forces were that had begun interfering.

It made me sad to ultimately lose a friend that I had felt very close to. In my college interpersonal relations class, we learned about determining whether our perceptions are true and accurate. How can a long-standing friendship disappear? The hard part was that I didn't know all the pieces of the puzzle. My friend had been keeping his true self from me, so some of the bumps in our friendship were caused by forces I wasn't aware of. To some, this would indicate he didn't believe I was his true friend, but I don't know what I could have done to change that. He didn't recognize me as someone he could trust. I always supported him, but that apparently wasn't enough.

Every girl feels great in her little black dress.

21.

Bowlers Know
How to Roll with Life
"Everything" by Michael Bublé

My best bowling moment wasn't exactly when I was bowling. It was when I was the bench warmer, waiting to bowl. I will never forget the feeling I had on that special day, when I was attending the high school regional tournament with my teammates. Often I dream about my first 225 game and the ultimate excitement of bowling a perfect 300 game. Oddly enough, I got a very special, unforgettable memory sitting out, bowling zero. Doesn't that sound strange? Let me explain.

The scene was the high school regional qualifying meet. As a freshman in high school, I was excited to have earned a spot on the junior varsity team. At the end of the season, the coach needed two alternate players to attend regionals, with no promise of participation, but to be ready in the event one of our varsity players couldn't compete. It was the sixth and last game at regionals, and so far I hadn't had a chance to bowl. I wasn't even thinking about that because I was having so much fun with my teammates. Unfortunately, one of our players hurt her leg and had to sit out. The two substitutes, Amanda and I, were both left-handers as well as freshmen. We were both having fun teasing each other about who would get to bowl. One of us would be chosen to substitute. Amanda got the nod and was going to take the place of our injured teammate. Then the moment came.

My coach came up to me and wanted to have a talk. I asked whether I was yelling too loud for my team because I would lower my voice. Or was I making too big of a deal about the beads I was stringing? I strung necklaces in recognition of marks and great plays my teammates were making. I made a necklace for each of the girls who were bowling. With every great play, another bead was added. I used different colors for different achievements, and different patterns for special spares or turkeys! It encouraged the girls to bowl better because all of them really wanted to have a long necklace. The longer necklaces proved we were getting closer to qualifying for state. I enjoyed making the necklaces because I felt I was really part of the team instead of functioning as a sitting out cheerleader.

Then my coach said, "Hold on for a second there. It's not about any of that. I wanted to tell you that I am really sorry that you are not going to get to bowl. You came to bowl, and I can't let you. It's just that the other sub has been bowling better lately at the last couple of practices." I realized this was true. Surprisingly, I wasn't as disappointed as I thought I would be. What a surprise that I came wishing for the opportunity to bowl, but I found myself feeling happy while sitting out. I glanced over at my teammates and realized how happy they were about the necklaces and waiting for me to come back and add some more beads. Then I looked at my coach with her sorrowful eyes and replied, "What are you apologizing for! I am having so much fun! It's an honor to be here! It would be an honor to do it again at state!" Then I gave her a hug. My coach chuckled and replied, "Why didn't you just say that earlier so I wouldn't feel so bad."

The last game was great! We didn't make it to State, but we all knew we tried our very best. My team was not as heartbroken as they thought they would be. They said they enjoyed the beads that showed how much they had accomplished.

My first year of high school bowling flew by. The season finished with Awards Night. Coach presented the MVP, high average, and all the usual awards. This was my first high school awards night, and I promised myself that I would work hard to earn a trophy in the next season. One trophy was left, and we were all wondering what and whom it was for. Coach called out my name, and I paused, wondering whether my hearing aides were working. She signed for me to come on down! As I walked to get my trophy for team spirit, Coach started telling the story of how she had to apologize to me that I wasn't going to get to bowl at the tournament and how I had started a new tradition of the marks necklaces. As she was talking, the sound started to blur and fade, as I looked at the faces of my teammates. I realized my happiness and precious memories came from being part of this team. Several teammates came up to congratulate me on the award. I replied, "Well, that's what friends are for—and, besides, bowlers know how to roll with life!"

Bowling helped me develop many memories. Dancing before tournaments, hosting meets, making banners for other schools, being excited for accomplishments of others, and appreciating others' recognition of my successes. For me, friendships provided the most important memories at the games. But, believe me, when I bowl that perfect 300 game, it will be hard to choose which moment makes the most precious memory.

By the way, today I bowled a 297!

E-A-G-L-E-S!

22.
Caring Bridge
"Someone's Watching Over Me" by Hilary Duff

One thing about living with a transplant is that, because of the anti-rejection drugs, it's easier to catch an illness, the illness lasts longer, and there can be complications. It's best to take care of things early, so transplant patients shouldn't wait as long as other people to go to the doctor when they have a fever, vomiting, or diarrhea. When I'm sick, I am careful to drink a lot of fluids so I don't get dehydrated, which makes my heartbeat fast and irregular. We aren't hypochondriacs; it's just that our immune systems aren't allowed to work the way yours does. A virus that puts you out of commission for a week can be disastrous for us. What could be a twenty-four-hour bug for you could set off a series of events that could have terrible results for me, like needing a new transplant or even death.

One year I had a terrible experience with a virus. It was the year that a gunman shot students on the campus of Northern Illinois University. Living in Illinois, I had many friends and siblings of friends who were there that day. Luckily, my closest friend, Rae, was ill and unable to attend class—the very one that was attacked.

The virus stuck with me; it just wasn't moving out of me. Crazy complications crept in: specifically, irregular heartbeats and extreme fatigue.

I was in and out of the hospital, actually a patient at several hospitals during this illness. To keep in touch, Caring Bridge offers a wonderful Web site at which families can create a blog to update and correspond with family and friends. When someone gets sick, it is hard to keep giving the status over and over. Many days, there is no change, just waiting, and family and friends want to know what is going on but don't want to ask and find out there is no progress. When hospitalizations turn into months, others go on with their busy lives. Through Caring Bridge, you can check on someone's status late at night after the switchboard is closed and before it opens in the morning. Your family and friends can post notes to cheer you up. There were many days when all I had to look forward to were the entries posted by friends that encouraged or comforted me. Caring Bridge actually helped me come up with the idea to write my book.

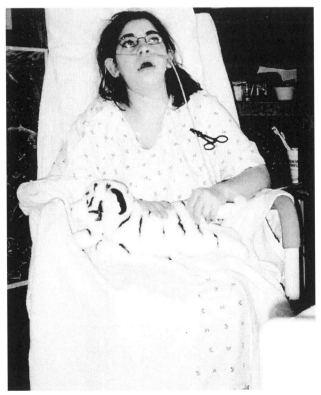

This is how I looked before my friends came.

These are examples of the things I said on Caring Bridge when I wasn't feeling well. I was fortunate to have people write back to me; they were the reason I had a positive outlook.

**Thursday, December 6, 2007
11:33 a.m.**

Hi, everyone! So I was supposed to have a stress test, and I was all ready to go. The cords on the monitors were hooked up to me. Then, all of a sudden, I was told that the schedule got mixed up. I had to get an echo done instead. While I was waiting to be wheeled in, I watched *Alice in Wonderland* for the first time! Then a doctor came in and said I had to have an emergency cath (surgery) today, at either one or three this afternoon. I said that I was looking forward to the anesthetic! I love how that stuff makes me go to sleep. It's much better to pass out from medicine than from a poisoned apple like Snow White! Donna is here with me too, and since I am not feeling well, I appreciate how she makes the day go by faster. I may need a stent, but if they find really bad stuff, they said I might need a new heart. If I need a new heart, I hope I get it from Paris this time, not Texas. Just kidding! I know a heart can't come from that far away. I'll keep you posted about what's happening! I have to go get ready. Talk to you guys later!

Love,
Snow White
Room 509

Because I was so sick, I had to quit my job, my one opportunity for independence.

**Thursday, January 3, 2008
12:08 p.m.**

Hey, everybody! Today is pretty much the first time in awhile I have actually gone out. I went back to Jacob's bowling after the holiday break. I was having heart problems while bowling, so I sat down and took a rest. Then I bowled the next game, and you won't believe it—I bowled my highest game, a 246! Yippee! I got six strikes in a row, and that is my record; last year I had five! I am looking forward to going to state in April with my Saturday night league. The best thing about this is that my team is really close. Our team name is "King of Queens" because there is one boy named Kevin; three "queens," Amanda, Katie, and Christine; and the princess Laia.

Well, the next doctor visit is January 11–12. That will be the major one that will tell us everything, including if I need a new heart.

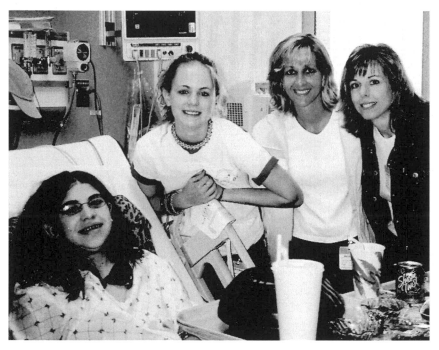

And this is what a visit from Abbi, Julie, and Jenny did for me.

I am sad today because of my health. I think I have to quit my job, which makes me mad. I know I can't help my health, but it's frustrating. Then again, I'd rather focus on school more than having a job. I did fine with both when I was healthy, but now that I'm not, I have to do what is best. I got straight A's again, whee!

Hope all is well for everybody.

Love,
Snow White

On Caring Bridge, it doesn't always have to be the patient writing on the blog; it can be a family member.

Friday, June 13, 2008
9:06 a.m.

Lucky Friday the thirteenth! We are awed and grateful for the family who donated the heart that has done so well for eighteen years! The question we faced this week is whether it is time to replace that heart. Although all the facts are not in, we support Lauren's decision to go forward 200 percent! This will most likely be a seesaw, back and forth for a while—it's time/it's not time. . . . We all know that this is a gradual process, and that we will go backward and forward in the next months.

If you want to do something, please talk to people about organ/tissue donation. If the unthinkable happens, we hope that individuals have considered organ/tissue donation and have talked with their family about their choices. If it doesn't help Lauren, it may help someone else.

We will probably come home later today. There is a problem with the neck site, and there will be an ultrasound today to determine how bad this glitch is, but it is likely the neck site cannot be used in the future. In addition, the IVUS and catheterization irritated the heart rhythm and caused a bit of heart racing. It was the first time I heard, "We might need to get the paddles!" This, plus an overflow of new transplants, kept us in the CTCICU (Cardiac Transplant Critical Intensive Care Unit) instead of the CCU (Cardiac Care Unit), which is just a stopping place before HOME—you can make up whatever those initials stand for! We will get this ironed out today, and get home and figure out how to catch up with school to take finals next week.

Thanks for your notes—Lauren appreciates them very much!

Janet

Sometimes, Caring Bridge can be used to send an encouragement to someone else, such as my Uncle Dan.

Wednesday, July 16, 2008
11:55 a.m.

Hi! Uncle Dan, get better! I love you, and if you need a balloon, I'll get you one! They were my favorite things to have in the hospital room!

This may be the last entry before I go to New York. The transplant cardiologist doesn't want to have a "date" with me until January! However, several other docs requested the honor of my presence in the coming weeks. Yesterday, I was very uncomfortable. I had to tell the doctor how I was feeling. I told him very clearly that I have been miserable, which makes me feel less self-confident about going to New York. They said the hematoma pain would take more time to disappear. I have lost even more weight. My stomach can't hold much food because of the swelling. I am looking forward to the time when the pain has gone away, and I am healthy to do the things I want to do! I am trying, but sometimes my energy goes down.

I still have to finish finals and read a book for school. I have a lot on my mind, but my body is telling me "go slower." Ahhh! I cut back on Safety Town; I tried to do two sessions, but my body isn't up to it. At least I get to see the smiles and laughter from kids like Faith. When I make kids like Andrew happy, I think it gives me courage about what I'm going through right now. I always appreciate the support of my friends and family, but especially now.

My plane takes off Saturday, and I really want to make it to New York because I want to know more about what would be a good career path for me after high school. Also, I'm looking forward to meeting people my age and experiencing the college life.

Love,
Someone who is stuck between a fairy tale and the real world

Fact of the day: I love the name Austin because that's where my heart came from—Austin, Texas! Pretty cool, huh?

Through Caring Bridge, you can tell people about a happy ending. For me, it was winning an essay contest and having the opportunity to experience college at RIT for one week.

Friday, July 25, 2008
10:24 p.m.

Hello! You are probably wondering how New York went for me. Well, *I fell in love with New York! I loved every second of it!* The classes were awesome. I took tests, and they recommended that I should apply to a four-year college. I was proud of myself for doing so well on the reading and grammar part, especially after being on morphine for weeks! You have to understand that, for a deaf/hard-of-hearing kid, English can be very difficult. I got to explore different career areas. Not surprisingly, my top two interest areas were social (the scale indicated I'm extroverted) and artistic. My counselor had a meeting with me on the last day of school. He suggested that good career choices for me could include an advocate, teacher, writer, or someone who works with medicine. He told me I was one of his most driven students, and they recognized I worked very hard in classes. He also complimented my mature character, my knowledge of my interests, and how hard I have been working to reach my goals. I told him that I want to use my life to help others. After classes, we got to go swimming, bowling, dancing, and meet 110 other prospective students. Some had cochlear implants, some wore hearing aids, and some had never learned to sign.

Now about the friends. I met the most guys ever in a short time period and was very comfortable with them because they were like me—they had hearing challenges. Four of us became especially great friends! Also, I had more boys than girls on my dorm floor (twenty-three male, thirteen female). The dorm was one of the best experiences I've ever had. The girls' half of our floor was decorated with Disney princesses! Oh my gosh, this was so meant for me! The other floors had other themes: *Alice in Wonderland*, *Indiana Jones*, *Wizard of Oz*, etc. The half of our floor for the boys was decorated with *Teenage Mutant Ninja Turtles*.

Among that group of twenty-three gentlemen, I did meet someone special. He writes very well, is Protestant, and goes to church every Sunday! The "someone special" looked so sad on the last day, and he told me in a beautiful letter that he was so happy to have met me, gotten to know me, and that he will miss me too (until we get back together next fall). He's a heartfelt and smart person, and we make each other laugh a lot.

Last but not least is the awards ceremony. Mr. Mark Sommers made a beautiful speech about my writing and mentioned my teacher, Ms. Rogers! (Ms. Rogers, if you are reading this, your name is on my plaque. How cool is that!) My plaque is for *first place*, and they took many pictures for the newspaper.

The last day was so hard, and I cried with my roommates. It's hard, knowing we probably won't see each other for a long time. We'll miss our close friends. It's amazing what six days can do. It was so hard for me to leave my friends. My closest suitemate and I loved dressing up for the parties. She is like my sister, and I miss her so much. Well, I think I got the basics. Ask questions if you have any.

Love,
Snow White/Lauren

This is the reason I went to RIT. It gave me motivation and a feeling of success after battling a thirteen-centimeter hematoma and a virus. I am grateful that I didn't need a new heart.

23.

College Life (Part 1)

"Numb" by Lincoln Park and *"The Long Way Around"* by Dixie Chicks

The summer before I left for college was a time in my life that I'll never forget. I knew I'd cherish the memories forever, because I was finally with a guy who liked me for who I am—and I have proof! Here is a letter he wrote for his application to film school. John had to write an essay about a real person who would make an interesting character in a movie.

> **John**
> **Film Major Essay #2: Real person as an interesting character**
> If I had to pick someone in my life that I thought was an interesting person, it would be my friend, Lauren. She is always cheerful and full of life. When I first met her, I thought she was normal, and was probably dealing with the same problems that all teenagers go through. Little did I know she was somewhat of a miracle.
> If you type her name, "Lauren Aggen," on Google, there are many links to read about her life story. When Lauren was born on December

22, 1989, she was diagnosed with a bad heart. Her mom told me that the doctors told her Lauren only had three days to live without a new heart. A miracle phone call came in. A baby boy in Austin, Texas, had died of SIDS. On December 29, 1989, at 11:59 p.m., Lauren's heart was removed from her body. On December 30, 1989, Lauren's new heart was put inside her, and her face started to look healthy again.

When I first met Lauren, she didn't really make a big deal about her childhood when I asked her about it. The longer I knew her, the more she started to reveal her past to me.

She has dark brown hair, the bluest eyes you have ever seen, and beautiful pale skin. I remember the first time that I noticed something different on her body. We were swimming at RIT, and she came out of the ladies' room wearing a blue bikini. On her stomach was a huge scar with thirty holes. As she swam toward me and popped her head out of the water, it was the first time I saw the scar from her heart transplant. I admired her for wearing a bikini and not caring what other people thought of her.

I asked her, "What's that scar on your stomach from?" She told me simply, "A tiger bit me." I was in shock, but then she started laughing and said, "Just kidding!" I actually believed her for a minute because the thirty holes did look like a tiger's teeth marks. Later on, she told me it was from gallbladder surgery. Lauren also told me that one of her best friends goes to RIT. I thought she meant her best friend, Kelsi, from back at home, but she meant Abbi.

I was very intrigued to hear more of her story. As we were splashing away in the pool, I asked her if there were any other medical stories from her past she could tell me about. She said something that included her past, all in a couple of short sentences. Lauren said, "Well, when I was eleven, I had my gums cut off of my teeth, and the doctors found a tumor in my mouth during that surgery. Around the age of sixteen, I had my gallbladder taken out. In the past month, doctors thought I needed a new heart, but the truth of it was that I had Valley Fever, chicken pox, and a thirteen-centimeter hematoma in my stomach from my annual biopsy. And then I came here to EYF at RIT a month later because I won the "SpiRIT" writing contest to EYF."

This is an excerpt from Lauren's journal the day before we went home from RIT.

> Dear God,
> Thank you for answering my prayers. I am finally over Andrew because I met a really nice guy at EYF. His name is John. I guess it is true . . . you meet many frogs before you find your prince. The disappointments help you appreciate the right one. For now, he's the one. I finally found someone who treats me well and likes me for who I am. He doesn't do anything perverted and is very respectful. He is funny, sweet, dramatic, smart, entertaining, loyal, and, best of all, he is pretty much just like me! We talked for hours at EYF about our similarities. We both love calamari, movies,

writing, and so much more! Can
you believe we've only known
each other for seven days! He
doesn't have blue eyes, but I could
care less about the eyes when it
comes down to his personality and
the way we get along. Who knows
what your plan is for us? When I
left EYF, John gave me a letter. I
wasn't supposed to read it until I
left the campus, but I decided that
I was going to read it to myself,
right in front of him! It was the
most romantic letter I've ever seen
in my life.
—Lauren

"I wonder how Lauren became so successful
at having a positive personality after having such
a hard medical life. How does she do it? She
makes it all sound like it's not a big deal: having
to get a biopsy every year, blood draws every
month, and taking twenty-five pills a day. I don't
know how she does it, but I guess I admire her.
To me, Lauren is an interesting person because,
even though she has told me many of her stories,
I always find out something new about her. This
is why she would be an interesting character,
because she is an inspiration and can be a role
model in many different ways to many groups of
people. Miracles do happen."

John did get accepted into film school, and I couldn't be happier for
him. I know he wanted to get in so badly, and he deserves it. Plus,
he wants to make my movie, but we'll have to see about that. I am
grateful to have a special friend like him. By the way, when I met him
at EYF, I was on morphine the whole time for the hematoma!

. . . .

I wish it was one world. At least that's how I thought it would be when I enrolled at Rochester Institute of Technology in New York—a school with a wonderful support system for those with a hearing loss. There are hearing, hard-of-hearing, and deaf students at RIT. What better way to go to a college? They provide mainstream classes and resources such as an interpreter, note taker, closed-captioning, and whatever else I may need.

Besides the support that the college provides, there is also a hospital two minutes away from the dorm that specializes in heart care. How much better can it get for me! Little did I know I would find myself feeling isolated.

I was placed in Ellingson Tower A on the twelfth (top) floor. Very interesting how they put a person with a heart condition on the very top floor; when the fire alarm goes off, I have to go down twelve flights of stairs. That's actually the easy part. The hard part is when officials let you back into the dorm after the safety check. I choose to take the stairs because I'm not going to stand outside in the cold waiting for the elevator with twelve floors of students. By the time I get back to my room, I feel good about the impromptu workout, and I can't wait to go back to sleep . . . in my single room.

That's right, I have my own dorm room due to my health. I am grateful for my own bathroom and tub. I decorated it with a black and pink Parisian theme and have a black and pink poster of Audrey Hepburn. Sometimes, I look in the mirror and try to pose like her— innocent yet sophisticated, all while pretending to hold a cigarette in one hand. I would do this as a warm-up for myself, like before having to take a big test or something. My room was small. I had a bed, a desk, and a whole stack of medications. I didn't realize having my own room was going to affect my self-esteem.

When I first moved in, I was very social and often went to people's rooms to chat. I enjoyed bringing company into my room too. However, after being suddenly immersed in a culture I was not used to, deaf culture, I began to withdraw as the year went on. My academics were fine, and I loved my teachers. It was my life outside of the classroom that I was not happy with. However, I do remember one time that my medications got in the way of my academics.

Due to my hearing loss, I have an alarm clock with a vibrating piece that goes under my pillow. When the alarm goes off, it causes the pillow to shake. I can't hear an alarm, but I can feel my head vibrating. Keep in mind, I don't have a roommate to wake me up in case I oversleep. Sometimes, my alarm clock would vibrate, but I would push snooze and go back to sleep. One day, I woke up and had only fifteen minutes to get to class. I dressed really quickly and walked out the door. It takes nine minutes for me to get to my classroom on the other side of campus. I ran and then realized I had forgotten to take my anti-rejection drug. I was debating what to do. I know it's important to take my medicine, but I had a paper to turn in—*a very important paper!* I ran back to my dorm, took the elevator to my floor, ran in my room, took the medication, went down the elevator, and ran to class. If you know me, you know already that being late gives me anxiety! I got to class late and was upset that had I disappointed the teacher. My classmates could see the tears in my eyes, and I suffered through trying to keep it together. I couldn't help being late due to my stupid health problems, and I felt sad that the teacher counted it against me. At the end of class, I let my walls come down and the tears fall. I felt alone and knew I needed to tell my advisor what had happened.

Little Women

Then the theater rescued me from loneliness. Ms. Luane Davis Haggerty, charismatic teacher of Acting 1, guided the class through activities that brought out an interest in acting that I hadn't been aware I had. The homework and class activities were so interesting, challenging, and fun! Sharing her love and expertise in performance art, I tried to develop my skills. This practice led me to try out for the play *Little Women* because I figured that I could play a little girl. I tried out by signing my true story of the coma that happened to me at age six. The director and judges were surprised and wondered how I came up with such a story. I was very nervous. Due to my trembling hands, sometimes if I sign for a long period of time, my hands will go into "shock." The next day, I found out that I was to be the understudy for Amy March, who was once played by the beautiful Elizabeth Taylor! I was so happy! I would be forced to learn more signs and would get to perform in one show, but that meant so much to me! At first, I loved that I could sign to my fellow cast mates and talk to the voice

College girls: Racheael, me, and Kelsi.

actors. As rehearsals went on, I sometimes felt caught in a political position: when I was interacting with hearing voice actors, etiquette would have me sign, and yet it was confusing to the hearing person in some situations when no one else was involved. I felt discriminated against in a sense, and realized it must have been confusing for the hearing people/voice actors, who are often interpreters, to understand that I could communicate with them in their mode—speaking. I was feeling insecure about where I fit into each group. I identified myself as not hearing, but yet not deaf. Someone told me I have always been a fighter. I'm not accepted 100 percent in either world. All I can do is take the best of each world and try to make it one world at times.

One night, the girl who played Amy March was absent. I had to be her. I decided that I was going to give it my all, and it would be my way of stepping outside of my shell. I'll never forget what the night did for me. Sick of being in two worlds and not knowing where I belonged, I decided to do what I do best—act. The director was shocked. She said to me, "Why didn't you show me that at the audition!"

That night, I grew up and began believing in myself. I think I proved that I had been underestimated, and that I had been underestimating myself. Under my picture in the program's cast list, I wrote, "Please consider being an organ/tissue donor. I wouldn't be here

Off to the prom!

if it wasn't for my donor."

The following summer, I ended up performing the role of Amy March in New York City! I had blonde pigtails and a puffy pink dress complete with a hoop skirt underneath. That was fun to manage! My dream role would be to perform the lead role in *Annie*, but I'm too old for that role now.

The Red Shoes

The actress who played the role of Beth March was going to produce her senior project after *Little Women* finished. When I asked her what the production was going to be like, she said it was a dance show called *The Red Shoes*. She encouraged me to try out, and when the time came, I did.

As it happened, there was a bit of a mix-up about the audition times. Posters on campus had the wrong date for the audition, but the Facebook page had the right time. I was the only person to e-mail Beth about the confusion regarding the audition times. And I was the only person who showed up on the first day of auditions! I was excited when I got four parts in the production.

However, after two rehearsals, I was cut from the dance team. The small stage only allowed a certain number of dancers. One of the most pressing problems for a young transplant, the necessity to keep health insurance, was also affected by the dance expulsion. The chain that is part of my life: in order to keep health insurance, I must be a full-time student. In order to be a full-time student, I must be registered for twelve quarter hours. Without the *Red Shoes* credit, I would dip below this requirement, thereby threatening my scholarships, my status for automobile insurance, and, most importantly, my qualification for health insurance under my parents' plan. All of this occurred, of course, on the weekend when I could not reach anyone to find out whether my credit could be earned in another capacity. The term pre-existing condition loomed above my head, with the knowledge that blood work, check ups, and tests recommended regularly would be beyond my means. The combination of personal disappointment, scholastic ruin, financial collapse, and spiraling health costs were a lot of pressure for a 19 year old. What a year I was having while many students from my dorm were out partying and enjoying what they were describing as the best, happiest time of their lives. No wonder I was feeling like an outsider.

Fortunately, I was able to pick up other hours working on other aspects of the performance. At the same time, I wanted to help Beth, and I told her to let me know what I could do to help. She sent me to a tall guy named Joe who was in charge of the crew for the play. He was cool, but, after he told me to help him lift a really heavy door for the set, I realized that wasn't the job for me.

From there, he sent me to the costume shop. I ended up helping people into their costumes, ironing outfits, and cleaning up the dressing rooms. I enjoyed looking at the costumes and knowing that it was my job to take care of them. Sometimes, if there was a really pretty outfit, I would hold it up to my body and imagine myself in it. At the end of a show, performers would throw their costumes at me; I felt like Cinderella picking up after my evil stepsisters. I'm glad this happened to me though—if I'm ever a performer on stage, I will never do that to a costume assistant! As a bonus, I was offered a job after the Costume Manager saw my work.

The show was in April, organ donation awareness month, and I asked the director to put an organ donor quotation in the program. He did, along with the Web site address for registration. I felt great pride in that because it was something I enjoyed doing.

The best thing I got out of theater that year was having my family come to RIT, not just to take me to doctor appointments, but to see me perform. My family gave me a Christmas ornament of Amy March to remind me to keep up the good work. I will cherish it forever.

In addition, I think often of the one friend I felt close to, the girl who played Amy March. Her father died because someone else drank and drove. She spoke about "Don't Drink and Drive" while I encouraged organ donor awareness. I thought that was cool of us, both freshmen, to speak up and say something to our audience, trying to emphasize information that could save someone, either way.

• • • •

I guess one of the hardest things about being immunosuppressed and going through your first year of college is making sure you take the time to fill all of your medication boxes and be sure you are taking them. If you go out, put a little pillbox in your pocket in case your plans extend beyond your medication time.

In my first year of college, I grew up a lot because it was the first time I was by myself. I couldn't wait to go home after my first year, and I wasn't sure if I was coming back. I had always had so much support, from my family and from people at the hospitals. Now, suddenly, I was out of my comfort zone. I really wasn't myself. My mistake was that I didn't go see a counselor, but, at the same time, I was doing a lot of growing up, as my mother says. She feels it's her fault because she never wanted to disappoint me, her baby. I don't think it's her fault at all. I know it must be hard for my mom to see me struggle, but I think she knew, in the end, that I was going to be okay. As I succeeded in new experiences, my confidence grew. I was determined that my sophomore year be better than my freshman year. The first year, everything is new; the second year, you know what to expect and how to change something if you don't like it.

My life adventure continues!

24.
May Angels Lead You In
"Hear You Me" by Jimmy Eat World

It is much more fun to go to a flea market with friends, because they may see something that they recognize, some trinket with which you have no previous experience. You would have placed no value on it, but they find value because of their experience. It is very interesting how several people can look at the same sculpture and have completely different reactions. After going to the movies, the discussion is always interesting as points that stuck with others are revealed. We each bring our own experiences, and they influence what we perceive. Discovering what others think comes with respect and a willingness to trust each other.

April 11, 2010

Being a little lonely in college, I began looking for service activities. At home, I worked with the National Kidney Foundation, the Illinois Eye Bank, and various community activities to promote donor awareness. I found the Rochester/Finger Lakes Eye and Tissue Bank had a community education division. Coincidentally, one area of the population they wanted to reach for awareness activities was the college-age population. Beside blood drives and poster campaigns, one other place I was asked to participate was judging a Donate Life Poster campaign. This opportunity helped me see the more administrative side of donor awareness activities. It was a new experience for me; in

At the Organ/Tissue/Blood Awareness Parade with Kelsi and Ashley.

the past, I would have been entering as an artist. New expectations and great anticipation enveloped me as I wondered what would happen.

The room had posters taped up around the walls, more than I had expected. We had come together for a common goal, but each of us came from different backgrounds. As we began looking at the posters, colors popped out at us, showing exquisite detail, exceptional drawing, and playful or soulful art.

The community education director, Karen, gave us instructions: "Thank you all for coming and representing different facets of organ/tissue/blood donation. Let's start by getting to know each other. Why don't you each tell your name and what connection you have to organ donation?"

Each told his or her name, and I learned one was a chaplain in the hospital nearby that had several active transplant programs. She met not only with patients but with families whose loved ones were potential donors trying to come to grips with sudden deaths. Another perspective came from members of families whose loved ones were donors. Participants included a nurse from a transplant unit, and three of us were recipients: one person received a kidney, one man received three corneas, and me, the heart recipient.

"The poster's purpose," continued Karen, "was to create awareness of donor registration for organs, tissues, and blood. So, for our first step, let's put posters that didn't acknowledge all facets on the table. We will look at these again."

Students from elementary school through high school had taken their time, developed ideas, added their unique style, and produced works of art that we were privileged to view.

This was unbelievably hard. Just as each person in the room came from different sides of transplantation, the entries represented students who had varying understanding of transplants/donations. Especially young elementary students might grasp one part of tissue/blood/organ donation, affected by what or how teachers had presented the contest rules, or because they have one personal experience. They each took the time to develop an idea, and create a work of art. This gave us time to consider each entry, as we collated this batch.

In the group, I met a girl my age who had recently had a kidney transplant. Very pretty and friendly, she had the kind of shiny, honey-blonde hair you see on models. She was tall and wore a short, tan mini-skirt with a white shirt and copper jewelry. I felt connected to her because of age and education, and because we both have had transplants. We were college students who were taking the day to see what we could do to promote organ donor awareness. I tried to imagine what it would have been like having a transplant at eighteen while still in school—the pressure of schoolwork, dating, being really sick, having surgery, and getting used to taking the anti-rejection drugs (and their side effects). Your face is different, your hair is different, even your skin color is different. All the while, knowing that you are lucky. Why? Because others die while waiting. And always asking, *why me*? Not *Why am I sick?* Instead, you ask, *Why was I lucky enough to get a match*? In my case, someone died. In the other girl's case, an uncle was the donor.

"Donors are heroes. Giving is beautiful." Reading the phrases, I tried to decide which poster grabbed my attention and educated. What is the right information? Imagine that you are suddenly faced with a life-and-death situation, and you are presented with an opportunity. Your loved one can't be fixed. I used to think that only happened in the movies or books.

Would the memory of any of these affect what happened next if the organ donation option was presented to a grieving family?

Among our group of judges, a perky young mom with pretty black hair and big hoop earrings was dressed brightly for the nice spring day. She had a captivating smile, and she was busy searching through the posters. Her aura was that of someone enjoying life—happy, lively. She was focused on the task because she had an appointment later. I wondered whether she or someone in her family had a transplant. She was sparkly, bubbly, and really kind.

I can't remember the ice-breaking question, but I discovered that she was here as a volunteer following the death of her son. As she introduced herself, she began to cry. "He was just twenty one," she said. Choking back the tears, she struggled to continue. She held her hand to her chest, stifled a cry, and in broken phrases continued. "I want to tell my son's story. He is a hero."

I wanted her to take her time. I wanted to be with her, appreciating what she had gone through after losing her vibrant son.

"He had been helping an elderly couple whose car had hit a guardrail," she said. "After he got them to safety, a car hit him. When I got the call, he was dead. Mangled."

The tragedy took my breath away. Twenty-one! He was a Good Samaritan. Bad things aren't supposed to happen to good people.

"Knowing Ryan, looking at what he was doing when his life ended—helping others—I knew he would want to be a donor. Unfortunately, the accident damaged his organs so badly they couldn't be used."

She paused, but then continued with a faint smile. "I was disappointed that no one approached me about organ donation. But a few days later, I got a call that there are other ways to donate. I was so excited." As we were judging, the mom recounted the call she got asking about donation. In my previous experience with organ donation, the donor had to be alive for organ recovery. At first, I felt shock—after enduring the horrifying news of her son's death and upon returning home, she was called about tissue recovery. She was quite excited about this.

"Even after death, the tissue can be recovered. I was so happy to know that Ryan could help. Now I know people can see and have better lives; Ryan would have wanted that. Now, two people can see because of his corneas; someone who had a terrible burn received a skin graft; and other tissues were taken to help others. I am so proud." Indicating the poster next to her, she said, "This poster speaks to me because it recognizes the gift. The donor."

I wanted to stop right then. Anything she wanted was fine with me. If there were a way I could bring honor to her son, I would do it. We all agreed that Ryan and other donors are heroes. They save lives!

"Dial Hero," a poster picturing a touch pad designed like an iPhone, showed where each application was an image of what could be donated. Another one of her favorites was, "Donors make dreams come true." Around the border were squares depicting different occupations that recipients might become when a donor saved them.

I wanted to listen to everything she had to say. I was so impressed that Ryan, at twenty-one, had been able to communicate his wishes to his family, that he had let them know he would want to help someone else.

"Jesus saves, and so can you!" (Did you chuckle when you read that?) The slogan puts the donor in very good company. The chaplain at the hospital pointed out that we don't want to exclude anyone because of religious beliefs.

There was another drawing, a self-portrait, by a boy in middle school. The image showed a dark-haired boy, and his chest had a heart drawn on the outside. It was accompanied by a short story of how he was born with a heart defect, and he had wondered whether he would need a heart from the outside. Some kids have to grow up with heavy baggage.

A bright yellow poster had a white body in the center with different organs, tissue, bone, and eyes—parts you could donate—colored in. It looked like the game Operation—childlike, but it quickly got the point across. I remembered hearing in art class that red gets your immediate attention, but yellow stays with you. This poster stuck with me, and I kept coming back to it.

We began to talk about the job of approaching families. Over the years, I have cherished the positive responses I have heard at awareness events. "Sign me up!" or "I registered at the DMV!"

With an unexpected death, or after weeks spent agonizing, waiting for improvement that doesn't happen, people may face that their loved one could live on in another way, by helping others. At Children's

Hospital, there was a deep blue poster with bright stars across the top. Curvy white letters spelled out "Don't take your organs to heaven. Heaven doesn't need them." A bright yellow poster with broken red letters read, "Kids need the darndest things. Heart, kidneys, livers." I was one of the lucky ones.

One poster had a very beautiful drawing of children in a circle, with one child in the middle. Each child was giving something— an eye, heart, kidney, liver, bone—to the one in the center. It communicated the point very well. The puzzle-piece concept was clever; however, it was similar to the autism commercials. Someone said, "I feel sorry for the kid in the middle; she's a mess!" But it did show that one person could help many others.

This judging was far more difficult than I had imagined. I thought the creative artist and winning entry would be apparent. However, the message came through in both words and pictures. One entry might have an outstanding drawing, but it might not have the right message or a complete message. Or it could have the wrong number. For example, one poster had "14,000 got tissues and organs today. 150,000 are waiting." That error didn't seem as important to me as the fact that the poster got the message across. Again, this was harder than I thought it would be. Couldn't we just change the number?

In fact, one person is added to the waiting list every thirteen minutes. The number waiting now stands at 109,000. Eighteen people die every day waiting, yet fifty or more people can benefit from one organ/tissue donor.

One judge was a grandfatherly type with bright white hair and shiny gold glasses. He was very proud to be the recipient of a cornea, actually three corneas. The first cornea lasted close to twenty years. The second developed a cataract, and he'd had his newest cornea for two years. I looked to see whether I could see a difference. One eye looked a tad cloudier, but I couldn't tell if that was the one with the cornea transplant or his other eye. He liked the poster done in black and white that had an illustration of hands offering a bright red heart with a charcoal eye in the center. There were no words, but the drawing was breathtaking. Giving the gift of sight or life in very powerful hands— so simple yet so magnificent that you can help someone see.

Now it was time to compare and eliminate. We each put a sticky note on any poster we liked, which fulfilled the goals. We put all the posters with no sticky notes on one table. Those with one or two sticky notes went on the next table, and three or more on the last table. Then the questions began: Does the poster include information on both tissue and organs? Is it visually appealing? Would it be memorable? Despite our different perspectives, we narrowed the selections to two posters—first place and honorable mention. Many of the posters swirl in my memory.

Several communities had entries, but there was just one entry from the suburbs. What motivated that one child to participate? Did he see something on TV or know someone who had received a transplant? Where did that elementary child find the information and get his idea for the poster?

• • • •

Donors are heroes. Donor families are to be admired. They are selfless; even in their grief, they are willing to help others.

The newest group of donors, live donors, can give their spares. Frequently, it's a gift to a family member, but sometimes the news reports stories like "Customer gives kidney to checkout clerk."

Another newer concept in organ donation is the paired exchange transplant. Maybe no one in your family matches, but you give a kidney to someone who has a relative that matches you—it's a trade.

Then there's the remarkable domino transplant. Say a man needs lungs, but his heart is fine. He receives a lung-heart transplant, with his heart going to someone else who is waiting. To date, the longest domino transplant chain spanned eight months, involved six transplant centers in five states, and resulted in eight transplants. This is truly an exciting development!

• • • •

A couple of weeks later, the Lilac Festival was held in Rochester, New York. Cait, the girl with a new kidney, mentioned she was going to ride on a float in the Lilac Festival Parade. She wondered if I was doing it too. I asked the director of Donate Life in Rochester if I could join. Before I knew it, I was decorating the trailer connected to a huge truck. Cait and I were the youngest organ recipients in the parade.

I had fun helping decorate the trailer with fake flowers, while others made signs that the crew would be carrying in the walk. The weather couldn't have better.

When the parade started, I was walking in front of the big truck and holding a sign that advertised "HEART–1989." Cait walked next to me and held a sign that read "KIDNEY–2007." We walked next to other sign holders, including Ryan's mom. "My son is a donor—2009." Behind the truck were people sitting on hay bales, also holding signs that indicated the year they received a specific organ or the name of a loved one who had donated. It was an amazing feeling walking down the street, with people watching from the sides and cheering loudly for us. Cait and I got into the spirit and shouted to the crowd, "Please become an organ donor!"

When the parade was over, I heard Ryan's mom talking about her tattoo, which I had first noticed when we were judging the posters. I didn't see the whole thing, but I heard her say the name "Jade" was inside a heart because she is Ryan's daughter. There were musical instruments on her arms to show Ryan's passion for music, and the lyric "May Angels Lead You In" from the song "Hear You Me" by Jimmy Eat World. From what I heard of the song, it seems to have been written to provide comfort to those who have lost someone.

Perhaps reading this book is a first step for you. Are you a registered organ donor? Knowing that unneeded tissue and organs could save twenty-five people after your death, I hope you don't pass up the opportunity to give someone life. Just think, you get a little immortality. Your life goes on.

One of my most fulfilling experiences at college was seeing people register after I set up an organ/tissue/blood registry information table at a theater event. Another student, Mike, from my American Sign Language Class, helped man the table while I was "in costume" for the performance and couldn't be at the table to answer questions. It was a good experience for him as well, because he could practice his signing skills with deaf visitors and speak to the hearing visitors. With his help, we made a little dent in the campaign to get members for the national registry and to educate people about this opportunity.

Frequently asked questions

1. Can they have an open casket viewing if the loved one is a donor? Yes.
2. Does it cost anything to donate? No.
3. What if my loved one has an illness or takes medication? The team will evaluate whether donation is appropriate at the time of recovery.
4. Are there age restrictions? No, organs and tissues are needed from people of all ages.

I am—are you? That was one of Illinois Donate Life's slogans. I hope you are, and you have signed up with the new national registry at www.donatelife.net.

25.
To My Donor Family
"Lullabye (Goodnight My Angel)" by Billy Joel

Dear Donor Family,

My name is Lauren, and I am from Illinois. You should know that there is not a big enough way for me, my family, or friends to thank you for what you did. It is by far the best Christmas gift I have, or will ever receive. That goes for my family as well. You didn't give me a box with a red bow on it. Instead, you gave me a chance to open those boxes with red bows on them. You gave me a chance at life.

I was welcomed into the world on December 22, 1989. Shortly after I was born, my face turned pale and my lips became blue. Eventually, doctors diagnosed me with mitral and atrial valve stenosis. One valve could be repaired, but not two. The doctors thought I would live about three days, but I could live longer if I had a heart transplant. Christmas Day was just three days later, and, without a donor heart that matched, there was little hope. However, I kept fighting and battling for every breath until December 29. That is when your family made the difference. Just after the stroke of midnight on December 30, I received a wonderful new heart. The amazing thing is when the doctor placed the heart into my body—they didn't have to shock the heart to get it going. It started beating on its own.

I am so very sorry that you lost your son. There are no words that can adequately explain how mysterious it is to me that this heart was unable to sustain him, but it sustains me. It took my family some time to come to grips with my needing a heart, because they knew, if a donor heart became available, it meant someone else had lost their precious child. The news of a possible donor was greeted by mixed emotions. Through each step, my family grieved in a way, trying to cope with the pain that your family would be experiencing. My family, church family, friends, and prayer chains all over the United States prayed for your son and your family, asking for strength and comfort.

I don't know how to tell you how grateful I am that, in your time of grief, you were able to look beyond your personal tragedy and generously donate your son's organs. I tell my mom that your son is my Prince Charming because he saved me. Truly, your decision saved me. Every day, I feel so fortunate to have been blessed with your compassion. Your gift has allowed me to become a funny, passionate, strong, and confident young woman who is not afraid to stand up for herself.

You might wonder what I look like. My nickname is Snow White because of my appearance. I have pale skin, dark hair, and big blue eyes. I wonder about your son, and whether we share more traits in common than our heart.

I don't know how to thank you enough for giving me life. One way to show my thankfulness is through the book I am writing—it's a memoir about the life you made possible. I have some goals in mind, and I hope the book will help accomplish them. First, the book is an attempt to tell the world how grateful I am, along with other organ recipients, for the gifts we have received. I think of this as public recognition of our heroes. After reading the book, it is my prayer that people will consider the miracles they can make possible by registering as tissue/organ donors. I hope that the information might bring some comfort and purpose to people when a loved one passes away.

In addition, I hope the book is interesting and brings hope to families whose children are facing transplantation. It is my intention to bring some joy to every reader.

I thought you might like to know a little bit about me; and I hope, after reading this, you are proud. Many things have happened in my life that would not have been possible if it had not been for your compassion. That's part of why I wanted to write my book. It may not be a typical journey, but, as my brother says, "It certainly is an interesting one."

I love to dance. Even though I have a profound hearing loss, I can still hear music. I love any kind of music! Carrie Underwood is my favorite artist. I worked my way up to becoming a dance instructor's assistant at a studio during high school. I love working with children. I love sports, just like my dad and older brother. Soccer and bowling are two of my best. I love public speaking, and I enjoy talking about organ/tissue donor awareness in driver's education classes. I am not afraid to stand up in front of a big crowd and make a speech.

I am currently attending a college in New York. I love it! I have a very cute boyfriend. I don't know if he's "the one," but he treats me well and we enjoy each other's company. I enjoy being involved with theater. I have made the dean's list every quarter so far. During my free time, I love promoting tissue/organ donation in the community. Every time I go to an event, there are usually older people with transplants, but, oddly enough, I have had my heart longer than they have had their new organ. They usually ask when I had my transplant, and I tell them I received a heart when I was one week old. They usually ask me again because they are in disbelief.

All my happiness is because of your family. I would've never been able to have any of these experiences if you hadn't made the decision to donate your son's organs. I was told you are from Austin, Texas. If I have a son, I'd like his first or middle name to be Austin, to honor and thank you. I have babysat a boy named Austin, and every time I see him, I wonder about you and what your son was like.

Thank you from the bottom of my heart. You have inspired me to want to help others. I feel so lucky and grateful that I got a heart and the opportunity to live. I know I was a baby when the transplant happened, but as I grew up, I heard stories about the event. I learned that I should live life to the fullest because it's the best way for me to show my gratitude to your family.

I will be putting this letter in my book. Please understand that I made up the story of what happened to your son; it's how I always imagined what might have happened to your baby, my donor. The book begins with a Christmas scene and a baby boy, happy and playing. A few days later, his tragic and shocking death is difficult to comprehend. At the end of the book, the scene will repeat. This time, the shock will be replaced by surprise for I am the mother now. This is to show that not only did you save my life, but also, because of it, life will go on.

With my sincere and deep thanks,

Lauren

26.
Kidney Failure

"Waiting on the World to Change" by John Mayer

My friend Alex had a heart transplant the same year I did; she received a kidney from her father when she was sixteen. Alex needed a kidney because anti-rejection medication had harmed her kidney, but her heart stayed strong. Just last year, I read in the newspaper that Bill, who was the first baby to have a heart transplant in Chicago, received a second new heart along with a kidney. It never really bothered me much, having a transplanted heart, because doctors told me my kidneys were okay. I always felt in my heart that my donor and I have been a good match.

This spring, I met Cait in Rochester—she got her first transplant, a kidney, at age seventeen. I wonder if we view things differently since she lived without a transplant for as many years as I have lived with one. My outlook may change now that my kidneys are starting to show wear from twenty years of powerful drugs. I'm taking one step at a time now. First, a change to drugs that are kinder to my kidneys without, hopefully, losing my heart. This means I would need two biopsies during the fall term of college. I was worried the biopsies would interfere with school, or worse, that I'd have to drop out because the drugs aren't working.

June 23, 2010

For the first time, I went to a kidney doctor for adults because Children's kicked me out, or "transitioned" me, as they put it. Dr. Bregman was the doctor that I was to see. I had met him before at an In-N-Out Burger in California when I was on vacation with my family. We were in San Francisco to see my brother run a marathon that went over the Golden Gate Bridge. I remember the day as if it was yesterday. . . .

Mom, Dad, and Dave were all eating burgers, while I was enjoying a vanilla milkshake at In-N-Out Burger. I looked out the window and saw someone talking on her cell phone. I kept looking at her because she looked so familiar. She was petite, with short dark hair, and she had her finger pressed to one ear, trying to keep out the noise from the nearby airport.

"Mom, is that Dr. Brown outside talking on her phone?"

My mom couldn't believe it. "Yes, it is!"

I went outside and stood in front of her, waiting patiently for her to finish. She glanced up quickly at my face, probably wondering what rude person was staring at her. Once her conversation ended, she looked up a second time, surprised and trying to place whom she was seeing a thousand miles from home.

"What the . . . ?" she screamed in surprise. "What are you doing here?"

"Having a milkshake," I replied. Then I asked her, "What are *you* doing here?"

We stood there laughing, not believing the coincidence. Because I was a frequent flyer in her pediatric practice, I was used to seeing Dr. Brown in her office, in "my" special room that had a life size Snow White for decoration. She followed me into the restaurant to see my family. As Dr. Brown chitchatted with my family, she shouted to her husband to get his attention, telling him that her "famous patient" was there. That's when Dr. Bregman introduced himself. Little did we know that I would soon become his patient!

• • • •

My doctors: Dr. Bregman and Dr. Brown. Was I surprised to meet you at an In-N-Out Burger 1,995 miles from the office!

A male nurse, José, called "Lauren Aggen" with a strong voice and waited to usher me into the office. He was huge and quite a presence in a navy blue scrub outfit. I could tell he was trying to decide who was the patient, my mother or I.

"Which one of you is Lauren Aggen?"

I proudly said, "I am!" I figured I might lighten his day a little because he probably dealt most often with really old people. He handed me a cup to pee in and was about to run through the instructions for urine samples, when I interrupted him with a smile and said sarcastically, "Wipe with the towelette, and then pee in this beautiful container!"

After turning in my urine sample, I headed into an examination room. The light was subdued, and the decorating was more blue than neutral, but pleasant. The medical assistant wrote down my vitals and recorded my current list of medications from the typed list I had brought along. The examination room had a model of a kidney. I had been looking at models of hearts for twenty years, so this was a new and interesting organ to inspect.

"Wow, I wish all the patients were as prepared as you are and brought a list of their medications with dosages," he said. "Many of them sit here thinking about the names and guessing at the doses!"

I have my current medications saved in my computer so I can update and print them for every doctor visit. I save them with the current date, and then I can look back to see changes in my plan. Having the information typed and available on a piece of paper makes the whole process go faster.

While he took my blood pressure standing and sitting, I filled time by asking the male nurse about his kids—you know me, I love hearing about other people's kids! Soon, Dr. Bregman came in with a resident doctor. After a consultation, he suggested that a kidney biopsy would clarify my status. Automatically thinking of a heart biopsy, I asked if I would be under anesthetic, and relaxed after he replied that I would be. He wanted to check my kidneys because the test scores don't reveal accurate information about the damage the anti-rejection medications have done. Unfortunately, or perhaps fortunately, I didn't realize that a kidney biopsy is different than a heart biopsy.

Heart: You lie on your back.
Kidney: You lie on your stomach.

Heart: The needle goes through the artery or a vein in my groin and up to the heart; other times, a needle is fed through my neck and down to my heart.
Kidney: The needle goes in your back, right into the kidney.

Heart: You go home the same evening after the biopsy.
Kidney: You stay in the hospital overnight.

Heart: Resume bathing in three days. Quick recovery.
Kidney: Two weeks of recovery.

I thought the first time I would get pinched in the back would be when I needed an epidural for delivering a baby. I guess my kidney had a different idea.

Here's how my biopsy went . . .

My main advice, if you are someone who prefers to have an anesthetic for a kidney biopsy, is to ask for the Michael Jackson juice! You are probably thinking that you don't want a drug that, although it will put you to sleep, could lead to death. Don't worry. My anesthesiologist said, "If you were my daughter, I would give you this kind of anesthetic." I knew right away that I was in good hands.

Before going into the operating room, I gave my mother my glasses and hearing aids. As I left, another patient, an older man, waved to me, probably thinking I'm some lonely kid in this adult hospital. I waved back for the fun of it.

The nurse wheeled my bed into the operating room, and then they asked me to walk over to the operating table. Guess what was the first thing I saw on the table? If you were guessing that it was the longest needle that I have *ever* seen, then you guessed correctly. I realized it was about to be inserted into my lower back, and I was so happy that I was going to get the Michael Jackson juice! Lying on my stomach, I heard voices but didn't quite know what they were saying. The faces seemed far away. I guess they didn't know, or maybe forgot, that I have a hearing loss and also can't see things far away. The talking mouths moved closer to my face, and I finally understood what they were saying. The anesthesiologist and nurses were just trying to comfort me. Because it is an adult hospital, they were probably not used to a young patient like me. I didn't even have time to enjoy the anesthetic like I usually do. Before I knew it, I was asleep.

Recovery two hours later . . .

I woke up feeling tired.

"Do you have any pain?" a nurse asked.

I barely wanted to talk because I wanted to go back to sleep!

There was a vague ache, so I nodded and put my head down. She put medicine into the lovely IV on my right hand (important because I am left-handed). I woke up an hour later feeling pretty much like myself—no nausea, vomiting, or headaches. A patient next to me was screaming and crying. I'm guessing she didn't get the Michael Jackson juice because I could see she was miserable waking up. That happened to me before with a different anesthetic. I soon realized it was the voice of an older lady, and I felt bad for her. She was probably scared and confused. I wanted to talk to her, to comfort her, but I couldn't because the red curtains between our beds were pulled closed for privacy.

In the waiting room, the nurse collected my glasses and hearing aides from my mother. When I was wheeled into my new room, there was a woman looking out the window. She wasn't that old, maybe forty. She had beautiful African-American skin, even though there were bruises on her body. I read her name, Ella, on the chalkboard information sheet. I love that name! I introduced myself, and we began to talk. She was very friendly and probably glad someone was there to talk with her. She told me that she had been in this room for three weeks! She had passed out at work unexpectedly, hitting her neck as she fell to the floor, but she was getting better.

Then it occurred to me to tell the nurse something important, as much as I enjoyed talking to Ella. "Excuse me, I don't usually share a room with another person. I'm immunosuppressed, so I've always had my own room." Thirty minutes later, I had to say goodbye to Ella and I was moved into my own room.

The room was old with peeling, peach-colored walls. Boring! However, I had my own TV right over my lap. The other bed had its own TV too, so my mom could choose her own shows when she stayed overnight with me. The TV was behind my bed, but I could pull it, and the controls, right in front of me. Not surprisingly, I took naps frequently. Between naps, I was fond of coloring; I gave colored pictures of Disney princesses to the nurses so they would take extra care of me! I know nurses enjoy getting a little something from their patients. At this point in life, I am glad I look young. Even though I may be close to the age the nurses are themselves, I can pull off being a young kid. Over the years, I've enjoyed giving my nurses things I have created, but this was the first time I thought that maybe I should act a bit more mature, because these nurses are almost my age. I don't want them to think I'm "special," but, if I'm on drugs, I guess you'll have to excuse me.

I disliked the pillow under the left side of my lower back that forced pressure on the mini-hole from the biopsy. It hurt, but I had drugs that made me sleep quickly.

I went home at noon the next day, and didn't think I would be in much pain when I got home. I know now, the recovery from a kidney biopsy takes longer than the heart biopsy. I am glad I won't be having a kidney biopsy often.

27.

Circle of Life:
Meeting Another Austin

"Send Me on My Way" by Rusted Root

Truthfully, it was so hard to walk. I would take naps often in the day, and sleep all night. The first week at home was rough. I didn't believe the doctor when he told me I couldn't bowl, but, when my league night arrived during the recovery week and I thought about picking up a bowling ball, I rolled over and went back to sleep. I had no strength and felt constant pain in my lower back—just the idea of bowling made me wince. The next week, I felt a little better. I realized distraction would help me to forget the pain, and helping children would make my inner self feel stronger. Therefore, I decided to help out at my church with vacation bible school. I know that kids can cheer me up, as they did when I had my heart biopsy in 2008 and worked at Safety Town after recovering from that awful hematoma. I don't want to sound like I'm complaining, but I must say, it was pretty bad.

Vacation Bible School, Congregational Church of Algonquin, 2010

Kimina's mom, Mrs. Jamison, was in charge of assigning people to groups. I figured I would work with the preschoolers or younger children because I can only do so much. However, I was put with the group of kids from fourth, fifth, and sixth grades. Each VBS (Vacation

Bible School) group was identified as an animal in the Baobob Blast program. We were the meerkats, and our group was given green shirts. I was surprised to learn that our group had to make the sound of our group animal. How am I supposed to know what a meerkat sounds like? I'm deaf! What is a meerkat?

"Mom, what kind of animal is a meerkat?"

"It was one of the animals featured in *Lion King.*"

"Thanks, Mom. That really narrows it down."

I was very stressed, wondering how I was going to do all of this. However, these challenges kept my mind busy.

I was assigned to Mrs. Rogeveen's station. She has the coloring of none other than my favorite, *Snow White.* Her daughter, Claire, is in the same year of college as I, and, although she is *not* immunosuppressed, I can't tell who's paler. Claire and I would alternate days, and on the "off" day I was assigned to help Mrs. Elliott. Mrs. Elliott is very energetic, strong, and fit. She has a son my age that, wanting to be trained as a firefighter, enlisted in the Marines. I pray for him at night, because he's on an aircraft carrier.

There were going to be ten students in my group.

It was time for music in Mrs. Janik's station.

"I'm waiting for a very important phone call," she announced one morning. "If my cell phone rings, I'll need to answer it, and Lauren will take over."

Oh great! The hard of hearing girl must teach music. Fortunately, a co-leader was nearby if I needed a back up, because I didn't know if I could instruct music.

The phone started ringing. When Mrs. Janik answered, she turned and said, "It's for Olivia." Olivia was the smallest of all the children, and she had the cutest laugh. She put the phone to her ear and got this priceless expression as if it was Santa Claus on the other end.

"Uh huh. Uhhuh." She stared wide-eyed. "UH HUH!"

She hung up and announced, "It was GOD, and he said, 'Study my teaching, and follow in my footsteps!'"

I looked at the troubled boys, who probably know the truth of Santa Claus, and gave them a stern look, as in "just go with the flow." Afterwards, we sang a song about following God's teaching and following in his footsteps. I couldn't help but giggle about the whole phone thing when I got home.

Another student, Andrew, was not too much bigger than Olivia and could be a model. He has a mole right in the middle of a dimple when he smiles, and he has beautiful skin. This kid made me want to do more than I thought I could. When I gave him praise, he accepted it and appreciated it. Little did I know, he's from a family of six kids, and probably liked the extra attention. After this vacation bible school session, I found out that Andrew had been in a bad car accident two years earlier. Of all his family members involved in the accident, he was the most affected; he lost his spleen and had to have several surgeries. Yet, when I looked at him, I didn't notice a thing. I will always admire him for his spirit.

I loved our meerkat/green group, despite not liking meerkats themselves. I don't think my students cared for them either, which made me feel better.

"Heaven is like a big Chuck E. Cheese's," stated Mrs. Rogeveen. What a great way to get the kids' attention and make them question, what IS heaven really like? I'll never forget that. Before I began working with this group, I was afraid of these kids' age because I was used to little kids. After being with this group as a teacher, I realized I like the older kids more! It's fun, yet you feel like you are getting back so much more than you give.

Vacation Bible School, First Congregational Church of Crystal Lake

Then the beautiful music teacher, Julie Janik, mentioned another community church was doing Baobob Blast the next week and asked if I would be interested in helping out in the neighboring town, Crystal Lake. Before I knew it, I got a phone call from a lady who was with the First Congregational Church of Crystal Lake, asking me to help out with kindergarten and first-grade classes. I soon discovered the group I was assigned to would once again wear green shirts, but this time we were the rhinos. I hoped this church didn't do animal sounds too, because I had no idea what a rhino sounds like! I didn't get it; a tiny animal identified the older kids, but the little kids were identified as big animals! Pretty funny!

Day 1

Word of the day: Trust.

Bible verse: "Trust the lord, and lead him to help."

Animal of the day: Zebras, because they go places together in a herd, in trust.

I got up early to drive to the other side of town and entered the white church. After getting my T-shirt and meeting my other co-leaders, I was sitting in the gym with the rhino section when I saw Julie with her twins, Colette and Cade. I love twins!

"Collette may be older, and taller, but I AM stronger!" Cade stated. Colette, who has the cutest smile, was in my group. Cade, the funny one, was in the other kindergarten/first-grade group. They had my favorite color, purple, on their shirts. I was okay with green, but I would have enjoyed purple.

As time went by, I looked over at the purple group next to me and noticed a blond-haired, blue-eyed boy who had an animal-print cover on his cochlear implant. I was really wishing I was in the purple group! I kept looking over at him, watching him sit very quietly until other kids in his group would laugh, and then he would start laughing. The gym was very noisy, and I think I was doing the same thing. Hearing aids amplify all the sound in the room equally. Therefore, the voices you are trying to understand are just as loud as fans blowing, lights buzzing, feet shuffling, and papers rustling. I would try to talk with the students in my group, but it was so loud, the only one I could truly understand was Julian, who sat next to me. He was the talker of the group, and loud, which was nice for me. I laughed when they did, bluffing to cover up my inability to hear what was being said.

I didn't know the name of the boy with the animal-print cover on his cochlear implant. But soon enough, a sign language interpreter came to assist him. At first, I considered telling the VBS director that I could sign, but I didn't want the interpreter to lose her job. Plus, I'm sure she was more skilled than I in ASL (American Sign Language.) I soon learned the benefits of having the interpreter, during gym time when all the groups gathered together. It was the one place I had a hard time hearing other people. Luckily for me, I watched the interpreter when the main speaker was talking. Due to my previous experience, I had learned all the songs with my green meerkats group;

I knew every song that we had to dance to. There was an option of singing, but I just lip-synced. Fortunately for the kids, co-leaders Brooke and Amy could sing the lyrics.

Day 2

Word of the day: Love.

Bible verse: "Love never fails,"

Animal: Monkey, chosen because their family is important and they are good at nurturing.

Just as I had the day before, I went into the gym to wait for my group to arrive. I saw this boy with the cochlear implant again, and I decided to sign to him. His mother, Mrs. M., was nearby, and she was surprised to see me sign. It's not like everyone at this church knew I was hard-of-hearing, because I came at the last minute. Colette knew I had a hearing problem, so she would talk extra loud to me when I worked with her one-on-one—it was cute.

"Hi! I'm Kim and this is my son, Austin." He was shy.

I signed, "You sign?" Actually, in ASL, it's "sign you" with a questioning look on your face. He nodded his head to me as his eyes opened wider in surprise that someone else here could communicate with him. I laughed, knowing how that felt, and knowing that Austin and I would have our own special conversations. I felt close to him; he was dealing with stuff that I had dealt with growing up.

As I watched him play with kids from my group, I saw him try to interact, but he didn't seem to participate as much as he wanted to. I thought he might not understand the directions. When he did participate, it was dramatic, sort of like how I am. Sometimes, he misunderstood the directions, but his interpreter would help him with explanations. I remember those days. It's hard to decide if you should watch the teacher, who is holding up examples, or watch the interpreter and miss whatever the teacher is holding up. Luckily, Austin's group frequently joined my group for activities because they are all the same age. This helped us build a relationship.

Austin's mom was one of the leaders at the game station. During this day's game, we stood in a circle while the person in the middle of the circle tried to make others laugh. When someone laughed, they had to go to the middle of the circle, and then they had to try to get others to laugh. I was sort of surprised when Austin came over and grabbed my hand to make a circle. It was probably just a coincidence, but then he signed "Hi" to me. He finally talked to me! Austin was in the middle as time went on, and I saw a kid push him. Little did that other boy know what he was in for. The shove led Austin to believe this must be a little tackle game, and he shoved the other boy to the ground. Another boy then shoved Austin, and he fell to the ground. He started crying, and I felt bad, but his mom was there to step in. He was over it soon though, and got back in the game.

Faith

After game time, Brooke (a leader) led all the girls to the washroom before the closing ceremony. I was at the back of the line holding hands with Hannah, when she let go because she saw another girl and wanted to give her a hug.

"Hi, what's your name?" I asked.

"Faith," she said, and then she hugged me. She laughed, and I loved her bubbly personality! Hannah and I resumed walking to the restroom but something wasn't right. I was having a Miss Clavel moment. (She's a character from the book *Madeline* who wakes up in the middle of the night thinking something is not right.) I turned around and saw Faith alone; she was not with a group and seemed lost. I don't know how I missed this when I first saw her. Hannah and I helped Faith look for her group.

"Faith, Faith, has anybody seen Faith?" when we saw a teacher coming toward us and yelling with concern. Faith gave me a hug before running back to her teacher.

"I'm glad that little girl found her class!" I told Hannah.

"Me too. She's my sister!" said Hannah. Funny how kids leave out things that they don't think are important. No wonder Faith wasn't scared about being lost and meeting strangers!

I immediately though of another sweet girl I had met in Safety Town. Another Faith was very special to me, and, because of her, I had more faith in myself after the awful hematoma. If it weren't for her, I wouldn't have flown to New York to participate in the Explore Your Future program at the Rochester Institute of Technology. She gave me the confidence I needed, and her name made me believe it too. I met her sisters, Sam and Gracie. I always think of them because Faith made a big difference in my life, and I never got to thank her in the way I wanted to, which would have been to baby-sit! If Faith or her parents read this, I just want to say thank you. Because of you, I have grown. I wish I had admitted at the time that I wasn't confident in myself; I was afraid that I could not baby-sit three girls at that point. I should have admitted that. I'm sorry.

Day 3

Word of the day: Follow.
Bible verse: "I will study your teachings and follow your footsteps."
Animal: Elephant, because they follow one another.

I wasn't at VBS on this day because I had to find out the results of my kidney biopsy. I learned that my kidneys are 40 percent damaged, but that's pretty good considering I've been on a drug for twenty years that is harmful to kidneys. I learned I would be put on a new medicine. However, I would have to get another biopsy in six weeks to see if it was working or not. In six weeks, I would be attending classes at RIT. I hoped I would be able to keep up with all my homework.

Day 4

(The last session at night)

While the kids were singing songs, I sat in the aisle in case Austin wanted me to sign for him, because his interpreter wasn't there that night. I will never forget when, at the end of one song, all the other kids sat down but Austin didn't. Instead, he put his two fists in the air as if he were Superman. I told my mom about it because I thought it was so funny. My mom said that I did the same kind of thing as a kid; except I'd give a princess wave to my brother while the other kids sat down or were getting ready for the next song.

Babysitting

Would you babysit Austin?" his mother asked me.

"I'll check my schedule, but I would *love* to," I replied. Because I have been dragging this guilt about not babysitting for Faith along since the summer of 2008, I realized this would be a perfect situation for Austin and me! Austin has a hearing loss like me, it could be pretty cool since we could sign *or* talk!

"Great. How about next Monday? My regular sitter is going on vacation, so I could use some help."

"I'll call you when I get home," I replied.

My surprise was that Austin has a twin named Walker! He also has a terrific sister named Aubrey. I really wanted to babysit Aubrey, Walker, and Austin; it helped that I finally was well enough to do it. A déjà vu feeling came over me when I met the rest of the family, I felt as if I was living inside the story I had made up about my donor family. I wrote the chapter "Temporary Home" months earlier, and this family was very similar—not the sad part, but the family structure. The first person I met was this tall, eight-year-old girl in pink pajamas. Mrs. M. introduced me to Aubrey. That was going to be a tough name for me to remember, because I'm so used to Audrey, the name of my brother's future wife who is like a sister to me. Aubrey was quiet and smart. I was ecstatic when I found out Austin was a twin—as you know, I love twins! When I met Walker, I never would have guessed that he was Austin's twin. Mr. Walker (as I call him) has curly, bright red hair, blue eyes, and freckles. This is in stark contrast with Austin's straight blond hair and evenly tanned skin. Walker is very much a people person.

Bloody Noses

The first time I babysat for Austin's family, I took them to the beach. As I was about to get in the lake with the kids, Mr. Walker came up to me with a bloody face.

"I think I got a bloody nose," he said calmly. He wasn't crying or upset. He said this with blood covering his cheeks and chin, and running like water from his nose. I loved how calmly Walker explained his circumstances. This contrast of the calm with calamity made me want to giggle. Walker has a wonderful, sometimes dry sense of humor. He wasn't scared, but he needed to explain his problem to get help. There was a lifeguard nearby who saw him and came over to rush him to the first aid station. Apparently, the sandy beach is a no-blood zone.

"It's not every day that I get a bloody nose," Walker commented as he held Kleenex to his face to collect the droplets. He looked like a mature salesman trying to sell me something. First Aid gave him an ice pack, which he held to the bridge of his nose. Little did I know this experience was preparing me for the future! Shortly, I would have to apply this technique to Aubrey.

Cleaned up, Walker had just jumped back in the lake when he saw a family of four passing a water football.

"Pass me the ball," Walker suggested. The large man looked at Walker, and ignored the young boy. As it unfolded, the family was pretty bad at the game, so he took a chance and threw the football to Walker, who had been waiting patiently in water up to his knees. Walker got so excited that he missed the ball, but he retrieved it quickly, regained his composure, and threw a nice pass to the man's wife. From that point on, the husband included Walker in the game.

The husband, looking tough with huge muscles, sunglasses, and a bandana around his forehead, was not as tough as he first seemed. Austin decided to get his own attention from the man by shooting a water gun at his chest. *Oh no!* But the man didn't get mad at all. The Harley Davidson–looking dude pretended that Austin had shot him, dramatically shaking his body as if bullets were hitting him. Then he put his huge hands on his heart and fell into the water. Austin was laughing hard, really enjoying the antics. I was enjoying swimming with Aubrey and her neighborhood friend, but I decided to pull Austin out of the "football arena" because I thought the man might be getting a little annoyed, even though he was still being nice.

Austin pointed to an area shaded by a raised platform that was near the deeper water. I understood why he liked it; the sand looked so cool and smooth in the shade. He gestured that he wanted to go over and swim. No one seemed to walk there, as there were no footprints from swimmers shuffling around. We swam around a little, and then we went to sit near to the stake that held up the square platform because it was shady there. Then a mother of a large family came over and gave us a dirty look.

"What don't you understand? The lifeguard has been blowing a whistle for a reason! Get out from under the platform," she appeared to be yelling with her face grimacing in frustration. Apparently, the lifeguard had been blowing his whistle the entire time. In her anger, she acted out enough that I got the point.

After looking at Austin, I noted his innocent confusion, but charming good looks. "We didn't know," I replied, "because we're deaf." Austin read my lips, I think, and he started laughing. I'm glad he wasn't crying or frustrated.

The lady looked surprised and mouthed, "Oh, sorry." Her expression changed to apologetic, and, as Austin and I swam out of the area, I saw her motioning to the lifeguard; pointing to us, touching her ear and shaking her head no.

The third time I babysat for these kids, Aubrey went into the bathroom.

"AAAAAAAAAAAHHHHHHHHHHHHHH" I heard a scream from the other side of the door followed by crying. Aubrey came out with a bloody nose—and not an ordinary bloody nose, but a really dramatic one. At first, she didn't want me to come into the bathroom, so I waited outside until she let me in. There was blood on the mirror, the countertop, the floor, and the walls, and there were blobs of blood in the sink. Aubrey had blood bubbling from her mouth.

You would think after my first-aid experience with Walker, or my own medical experience, I would be fine. I can deal with stuff like vomit, shortness of breath, high or low blood pressure, IVs, or any type of epi-pen that needs to be stabbed into a child when they have an allergic reaction. However, I'd never really had an experience with a bloody nose like the one Aubrey had.

I put an ice bag on her nose as they had done for Walker at the beach, but this girl would not calm down. On the other hand, I was very calm—this wasn't exciting enough for me. (Yeah, right!) Of course, I had to face my fear of failure as a babysitter and call her mom and grandparents to see whether this was unusual. No one answered. I called my mother because I was really concerned about Aubrey. Aubrey had been sick with a fever before the bloody nose. What I didn't know was that Aubrey is prone to bloody noses, and I should have called her dad. I had tried him once before, but he didn't pick up because he didn't recognize my cell number. He was expecting a call from the house, but didn't realize that I can't hear on some regular phones, so I automatically use my cell. Lesson learned.

After all my transplant checkups with stress tests, biopsies, cardiac caths, blood draws, etc., I still wasn't prepared for a bloody nose incident. By the time my mom arrived with popsicles, Aubrey was fine, and I was proud that I had taken care of it, thanks to the preparation with Walker. The popsicles Mom brought put a happy ending on this dramatic bloody nose story. Turns out, Aubrey liked blue raspberry best, just like me!

Baseball

Walker, Austin, another neighborhood boy, and I started a game of baseball. At first, Austin didn't want to play, but once he saw that I needed someone else on my team, he joined. Walker was very good at making the calls.

"Ball one!"

"Strrrrrrike!"

"Foul!"

Austin sheepishly, at first, joined in. He understood the parts that mattered, right away. For example, it mattered to him to look the part by wearing a mitt when he was the pitcher. It mattered to him to have a ritual of patting the bat on the ground every time he was up to bat, just before he got ready to hit. I remembered that I had a pitching ritual when I was his age. I lifted my knee really high when I pitched, and would turn around to spit before throwing the ball.

During the game, Walker's teammate yelled and pointed to Austin who was standing on third base.

"Run to second!" He pointed from third to second base. The kid had the ball in his own mitt. Trusting the neighbor, Austin followed the directions because he didn't know much about baseball. As he was running, the kid tagged Austin and Walker yelled, *"Out!"*

Austin was hurt, confused, and upset.

"That wasn't fair. A friend doesn't trick someone into running the wrong way," I lectured.

"We're up," yelled Walker. "It's our turn to bat," he pleaded, accepting that the out was the result of Austin's mistake.

"Hold on," I said. After my explanation, Austin returned to third base, and Walker let me bat so Austin could run home. I knew it mattered to Austin that he advance to home plate. I hit the ball far to give him enough time to run, and I let Walker tag me out so Walker's team could get their turn at bat. In the end, everyone had fun and that was all that mattered. Afterwards, I checked on Aubrey who was having fun talking with the other girls from the neighborhood. Bloody nose stopped. Blood cleaned up. All in all, it was a good day.

Bedtime Stories

My favorite time babysitting was reading bedtime stories. This should be no surprise due to the impact my grandfather had on me with his creative storytelling. I loved getting into the drama of the stories, using dramatic facial expressions that I practiced in acting class with Ms. Luane Davis Haggerty.

I read to Aubrey first so she could go to bed quickly; she wasn't feeling well. Aubrey wanted me to read a particular book to her before she drifted off to sleep. I wished I could take Aubrey's sickness away. I'm so used to being sick that I wouldn't mind being able to taking it away from a child. When I started reading the story to Aubrey, I got nervous because I noticed all the "s" words in the tale. Instead of doing my dramatic storytelling, I focused on my speech and practiced saying the "s" sound. I wanted Aubrey to be able to understand me.

After my "speech therapy" with Aubrey, I read a book to the twins in Austin's motorcycle-themed room. Of all the books on Austin's bookshelf, Walker picked a story about ambulances. Go figure, something I really know about. I had so much fun showing the twins my dramatic facial expressions. I found it funny that they kept looking at my face instead of the book. If I said a word really loud, Austin would repeat it after me. Afterwards, Mr. Walker would tell me an informative fact about the word.

After I put Austin to bed, I went with Walker to his sporty bedroom. Mr. Walker really wanted me to read him one more story before going to bed—something about a pig with pancakes. After reading the very short tale, he wanted me to listen to his story about his experience with pancakes. I listened and then tucked him in for a good night's sleep.

• • • •

There's always a reason why we are where we are. We might not know it right away. For me, knowing what it feels like to be deaf, connecting with Austin gave him a chance to express his feelings in a mature way, while also helping others who couldn't relate to his challenge to understand. I wanted Austin to watch and learn. I felt proud when

Walker stood up for Austin, when he let him run to home base because he understood that his teammate had tricked his brother. I was proud of Walker for telling Austin, "You're not out," and that was the best call he made all day. Walker is an advocate for Austin, and I think that's cool. I hope when the boys are in high school, that they are still good friends. I wish I had a twin, someone to look out for me; I'm happy that Walker is going to be that person to Austin. In the end, I know Walker will learn things from Austin as well. I think Austin will be an inspiration to Walker, if he isn't already.

• • • •

I thought it was a coincidence that the children in my chapter "Temporary Home"—written months before I even met Austin—were similar to the kids I babysat, and that Austin, the one I babysat, was like me.

Austin Gift Donor Family (Fictional story)	Austin's Family (Babysitting)
Youngest son:	Youngest son:
Austin with blue eyes	Austin with blue eyes
Three children in household	Three children in household
One girl, two boys	One girl, two boys
Twins: Morgan and Tommy	Twins: Walker and Austin

If it weren't for Austin (the one I babysat), I wouldn't have had faith in myself about going back to college where there are two worlds. I want so much for it to be one world, not divided into hearing and deaf. If it weren't for Austin (my donor), I would never have met these great kids.

I guess when I saw Austin going through challenges similar to mine, it felt like the circle of life. While I was helping Austin, he was helping me at the same time. I feel like I was meant to meet Aubrey, Walker, and Austin. If I hadn't, I wouldn't have become stronger after my kidney biopsy. I also wouldn't have had the opportunity to write about them. If it weren't for those kids, I wouldn't have my favorite memory of John, when he visited me in Chicago and we had so much fun babysitting that he extended his stay! After a hard first year of college, it was nice for him to finally see the real me doing something I love. It was nice for Austin to meet a grown-up—i.e. John—with a cochlear implant.

You might wonder if I ever thought of Austin, the kid I babysat, as my donor. While I never did, the name reminds me to be grateful and encourages me to think of others' challenges. Austin is a sweetheart and can make my bad day into a good day. Plus, he's really cute and cleans the house!

• • • •

The best part of having experienced VBS is that now, when I go to church and see some of my students, I get to catch up with them. I had been hoping to run into Andrew before he moved to Nashville. Then I saw him lighting the candles in a white robe, looking handsome in his new glasses!

This summer, at the Algonquin Founders Day parade, I sat watching as the Boy Scout float passed by. There was this short boy walking with the float and talking to friends. I didn't think anything of it until he turned toward my side of the street to throw candy. There he was, all dressed up and still smiling with his delightful spirit. I screamed, "Andrew!" I felt like I was a fan at a rock concert screaming the musician's name. He couldn't have had a better reaction. He was surprised, his mouth wide open. He started waving at me, double-checking to make sure he was waving at who he thought it was, and I laughed. I read his lips as he told his brother (who was marching with him) that it was "Miss Lauren." He remembered me!

Just when I thought my day couldn't get any better, I saw a boy with dark hair, pale skin, and bright blue eyes. I gently tapped him on the shoulder and walked past. At first, he looked to see who tapped him, and then he shouted, "Lauren!" and ran to give me a hug. It was Eric, another boy I enjoy talking to because he always has something to share. I love the older kids and wish I could work with them forever. I saw Mrs. Rogeveen, who was her usual perky self.

These are the people I live for—those who need my help in any way. In this way, I can show my gratitude to my donor family. I want to make a difference, even if it's just making a kid smile. When I went back to school, I posted pictures of the children I worked with this past summer on my wall in my dorm room. They are my constant reminder to not give up as I face the unknown challenges of my second year at RIT.

28.
College Life (Part 2)
"Jai Ho" from Slumdog Millionaire

Before I knew it, I was packing in my room to get ready to go back
to RIT. One thing that really made me want to return was that I had
been offered a job! If it wasn't for the student director letting me go,
dismissing me from the cast of her play *Red Shoes*, I would never have
helped out as costume assistant, and then I would never have tried
to work in the costume shop. This connection led to the job in the
costume department! When one door closes, another one *does* open!

During high school, I got a job at the library. It lasted only
three months, because I had to quit due to a severe virus and its
complications. As a consequence, I have always worried how I could
keep a job when I get sick all the time! I was anxious to get to work
at my job, because that would take me away from the problem of
"socializing with people," and my self-esteem would go up, knowing
I was actually doing something constructive, even if it was making
costumes.

Costume Shop

It has been so pleasant to work for someone who understands
about my health. Damita has been more of a friend than a boss.
I could always go to her, and talk to her just about anything. The
director from *Little Women*, Luane Davis Haggerty, is that kind of
person to me too. Two other students will be working alongside me.

Laura, who is very intelligent, is an animation/film major. Sometimes I get confused, wondering whether Damita is calling for Lauren or Laura. Laura is very confident, and I know I can always go to her if I need help. She is very artistic, yet stubborn at the same time—kind of like me.

The other co-worker, Steve, looks like Howie Mandell, and is such a sweetheart! He has black-rimmed glasses that make him look like he belongs in the costume shop, as if he was a fashion designer. Steve lost his hearing five years ago, and decided to get a service dog. BeBe, a black lab, is always with him, and is so cute! I learned I couldn't touch BeBe when her orange working vest is on, because the vest signifies that she is working and because it would be bad if I distracted her when she might need to warn him. She may play when the vest is off. Then she becomes so playful and loves to fetch a ball. I call her baby, yet she still knows I'm talking to her. Eventually I learned not to call BeBe anything, because she's at work, just as I am, perhaps sewing a button on a jacket.

One day, I was scheduled to work for four hours. Damita asked me to wash and rinse a long, curly, ratty brunette wig. Then she wanted me to comb out all the tangles. After brushing out this long, twisted wig, I developed a greater appreciation for my mother, who spent hours brushing out the tangles in my hair when I was little. I couldn't help that my hair was so thick and tangled, due to the drug Cyclosporine. My ponytail had been so thick, my mom couldn't twist the band more than once! We tried so many products—detanglers, relaxers, and frizz-away products.

I remember crying, kicking, and screaming when my mother brushed out my hair. She often referred to it as a rats' nest. I had a hard time doing it myself, so I needed her help. Sometimes I don't think my mother was really hurting my head, but I was probably tired of sitting in the bathtub, knowing the brushing would take a while. So here, at my new, favorite job, I recognized what she must have gone through every day. No wonder my hair looked like Roseanne Roseannadanna from Saturday Night Live!

My favorite thing to do at my new job in the costume shop is to dye fabric! It has brought me comfort knowing I could use a mask and gloves, which are required for safety regulations. I learned different ways of tie-dyeing shirts with all sorts of patterns. It is so much fun!

Hanging out with Kimina!

Before I knew it, I was working on my own costume, for my role in a play directed by Bonnie Meath-Lang. *Inherit the Wind* was the first play of the season. And my voice actress for the play was Cait, whom I introduced to you in "May Angels Lead You In." I figured this would be a nice opportunity for her to do something while she was out of school because of having knee surgery. During the show, Cait and I decided to give everyone in the audience a bracelet that promotes organ donation awareness and registration. It's nice to see how this all came together.

During rehearsal one day, people pushed me into an audition room. It was for a dance show called *Danser et Voler!* Apparently it means to dance and to fly. I felt distressed returning to the same room where I practiced for *The Red Shoes.* I didn't want to try out for another dance performance; I was afraid I'd perform poorly. But there were all these people encouraging me to try out. For some reason, I felt I couldn't back out. There I was, standing in a line with tall skinny ballerinas, contrasted with me—short, wearing jeans, a shirt, and socks. It wasn't like I was prepared to dance. Then a familiar face walked in, and it was Sam from *The Red Shoes.* It was nice knowing that I knew someone, and she was even nice enough to lend me her dance shoes, because I didn't have mine with me. At that moment,

I was glad I had tried out for *The Red Shoes*. Still, I felt insecure, wondering what Sam thought of me as a dancer. I didn't want to embarrass myself, knowing she knew that I was one of the people cut out of the previous dance show.

I thought I didn't have a chance of making it, so I told the director, Thomas Warfield, that if he needed other help with the production, whether it was handing out programs, painting scenery, or costumes, to let me know. I really admired the dance instructor, who reminded me of Willy Wonka. He has been recognized for his efforts to make the world a better place. Mr. Warfield was honored for his ability to encourage diversity, through, in part, his determination to unite groups in dance troupes. On a broader level, he devotes times and action to promote peace and understanding through workshops, performances, and networking. Besides RIT's *Isaac L. Jordan Diversity Award*, he was recognized as an *Unsung Hero* by the Rochester community. He is not only an inspiration and a model for humanity, but exudes a calm yet strong drive that makes each person want to do better. I appreciate his magical spirit in life. He is often connected with something purple: either the pen he uses to jot rehearsal notes, or perhaps something in his attire. His office is filled with plum-colored objects, and I was surprised to find his office door was a vibrant purple in an environment dominated by the color orange. When he teaches, I feel that all my bad thoughts or worries disappear as I concentrate on movement. I feel like a dancer in Neverland with Thomas Warfield revealing some magic in life, just as Peter Pan had. He is always patient with me, because I will admit, I'm not like the other ballerinas, who are talented at spinning and keeping their balance as their long legs extend gracefully into the air during their leaps. Through his efforts, I expanded connections with people I may have never have had the opportunity to get to know during my hectic college studies. I do enjoy becoming aware about the things to which I had never given thought, nor experienced before.

After the tryouts, I thanked the circus lady for being a wonderful teacher. For part of the audition, we had to try tumbling things. Being the shortest person in the room, I was used as an object that the long-legged ballerinas could leap over. However, I must say, I did well when it came to jumping on a trampoline.

The following night, I received an e-mail that told me I had made the first cut and it was mandatory that I attend the second part of the dance audition on Saturday. But on Saturday I was supposed to go to Canada to a roller-coaster park with a group of friends from *Inherit the Wind*. I felt so torn, because this trip was the one thing I had been looking forward to while struggling to find a social group during my first year at RIT. I was finally going somewhere with a group of "friends" without John. It was my chance to get to know them on my own. Now I had to tell them I couldn't go because I wanted to complete the second part of the audition. Plus I really wanted to learn from the talented dance teacher, Thomas Warfield. After the second audition, being dressed appropriately, I found out later that evening that I wasn't an understudy, but actually part of the cast. I didn't jump in the air, I just stood there, and thought about everything I went through with *The Red Shoes* and other bad theater moments, and how it came down to this. I walked in the hallway, back to my dorm, just stunned. I was speechless. I felt honored making the cast. No, I may not be a ballerina, but I have character, and maybe that's what did it!

Medical

In my second year, I am better at advocating for myself, especially now that I have access to a car. I experienced many challenges for the first time last year, which is why I probably felt so isolated. Now, for the first time, I drive myself to the hospital if I'm sick, and go to Wegman's (famous Rochester store that is the best grocery ever!) to pick up my prescriptions. However, I miss having my mom, Aunt Donna, Dad, or Dave to talk to while waiting in the doctor's office. Instead, I do last-minute homework or catch up on my readings for class.

Throughout my life, I haven't had a true opportunity to advocate for myself when it comes to transportation, or calling in for a doctor's visit. And there's that annoying voice in the back of my head, telling me that I have to go back to doing school work and get all caught up in my classes. After I do catch up, I feel that is a success in itself.

Thanks, Mom, for doing all that you continue to do; and thanks for letting me grow up and take on more responsibility for myself. Wait, did I say I *want* to grow up?

Mom and me—best friends forever!

That's why I struggled so much my first year, because it was all new to me, and I was looking for security that my mother had always provided for me. I have my days in which I am mad about my medical life, but I get over it, because now I have things to do! I see a counselor when I get really stressed out, and I'm glad I know now how to get help. I am taking an ASL 2 course, to help me communicate better with those who sign. I also plan on going to speech clinic to improve for the sake of my future career.

There is still that question: what it is I want to do in life for a career? I am still struggling with that, and hope to find the answer. My health does get in the way of making that decision, and sometimes that is hard for me to accept. I won't be working in an office with sick children, or standing on my feet all day. It does bother me, because I wish, like some people who are confident in their career goals, that I knew what would be my perfect career. For me, I am taking pride in managing going to hospital appointments, and overcoming the time lost in which I can keep up with classes.

29.
Conclusion?

"Don't Forget to Remember Me" by Carrie Underwood and *"What a Wonderful World"* by Louis Armstrong

I know I am ending this book abruptly, but I am a work in progress. I wanted to get my story out now, so people might start considering how they can help others. I am aware that many people already have, in many different ways, and that is fantastic! Through this book, I hope you gain a little understanding of how important donors are.

Imagine, one donor can save more than 50 people from suffering.

Every thirteen minutes, someone else's name is added to the waiting list. Every day, eighteen people die because their needs could not be matched.

My sincere wish is that you never have to face such a circumstance. But, if you do, I hope a donor will come forward for you.

Having gotten to know me a little, you know that, just like everybody else, I'm trying to find my way on my life's journey. Future plans can seem overwhelming at times, but each day I am grateful for the chance to face the challenges and the joys and work through the set-backs. Perhaps my accounts made you laugh a little or maybe cry sometimes, but hopefully you enjoyed this reading experience.

I hope you have talked to your family about your feelings about tissue/blood/organ donation. There are many opportunities to help

At the beach!

others. Just last week, I found another way to help: I got my hair cut for Locks of Love!

One thing I do look forward to is the day at RIT when my parents can see me graduate. I have never been part of a graduation ceremony before! In middle school, I became very ill on graduation day, and I missed the opportunity of receiving not only my diploma but the Citizenship Award for public and community service. In high school, I ditched my graduation, to go to prom in New York. This time, I hope I am able to make it to my graduation ceremony at RIT. I want to do it for my parents. They deserve to see such a day for their Christmas miracle daughter. I recently found out I will be the college delegate for

NTID. This means I will be one of eight students who actually go on the platform and accept a diploma for their branch of the college.

I hope one day to meet a real nice man that I can go on a lifetime full of adventures with and know in my heart that he appreciates me for who I am! Right now, I am learning what I want out of life, and learning to understand the world and where I fit in. Who knows where/what happiness lies ahead? Wherever I land, I will always try my best to stay true to my heart.

30.
Movie Dream
"Hollywood" by Madonna and *"Let Go"* by Frou Frou

My dream is to continue to encourage others to consider being an organ/tissue/blood donor by producing a film based on this book. I've always dreamed that Steve Martin would play the role of my father. Indeed, my father is very similar to George Banks (from *Father of the Bride*).

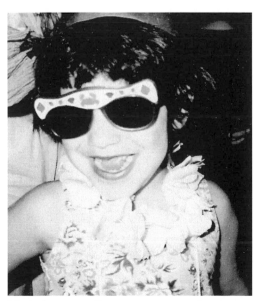

Movie dreams . . . from a very young age!

In my vision, the movie starts with a scene of a family's first Christmas with their newborn son, Austin. The next scene would take place three days later, and you would see and hear the mother cry out as she enters Austin's room. At the end of the movie, I would like to see the exact same scene of a mother going into her baby's room, but this time, the mother comes out holding her baby in her arms. When the camera zooms in on the mother, it is me, all grown up. It's Christmas, and the twins are pulling my robe, begging me to come downstairs and open presents. This is to show that Austin not only saved my life, but he made it possible for life to continue, through me.

REFERENCES

Aggen, David H. 2010. "Engineering Human Single-Chain T Cell Receptors." Diss., U of Illinois at Urbana-Champaign.

Stickney, Doris. 2010. *Water Bugs and Dragonflies: Explaining Death to Young Children*. Cleveland, Ohio: Pilgrim Press.